"The faculty for telling stories to children is relatively so rare—and the value of really good stories so great (is this why they are so rare?)— that one gives a ready and a hearty welcome to the Sister of Notre Dame who has recently enriched our limited supply with *True Stories for First Communicants*. Not all folk savor alike in such matters; but it really seems as though everybody ought to like these stories. First because they are true—true to fact: to past history and to present-day experience. Secondly, because they are fresh and bright—what children like. They are not meant to scare. They are not exaggerated. They are sensible, simple, sweet. They make good reading for children of every age—young children and old children."

—*American Ecclesiastical Review*, November 1919

"Come down, Little One.   Here I am."

FIRST COMMUNION DAYS

TRUE STORIES FOR FIRST COMMUNICANTS

BY

JULIE DU ST. ESPRIT

A SISTER OF NOTRE DAME

2019

ST. AUGUSTINE ACADEMY PRESS
HOMER GLEN, ILLINOIS

This book combines two titles under one cover.
It has been newly typeset based on the edition of *True Stories for First Communicants* published in 1949 and reprinted in 1956 by Sands & Co., and the edition of *First Communion Days* published in 1920 by B. Herder. All editing strictly limited to the correction of errors in the original text and minor clarifications in punctuation or phrasing. Any remaining oddities of spelling or phrasing are as found in the original.

TRUE STORIES FOR FIRST COMMUNION

Nihil Obstat

GEORGIUS CANONICUS MULLAN

Censor Deputatus

Imprimatur

HENRICUS G. GRAHAM

Epus Tipasitanus

Edimburgii, die 28 Feb. 1919.

FIRST COMMUNION DAYS

Nihil Obstat

ROBERTUS E. BROWN, S.J.

Censor Deputatus

Imprimatur

HENRICUS G. GRAHAM

Epus Tipasitanus

Edimburgii, die 10 Martii 1920.

These books were originally published in 1919 and 1920, respectively, by Sands & Co.
This edition ©2019 by St. Augustine Academy Press.
All editing by Lisa Bergman.

ISBN: 978-1-64051-074-6

All illustrations in this book are the original illustrations by Wilfrid Pippet.

CONTENTS

TRUE STORIES FOR
FIRST COMMUNICANTS

FIRST COMMUNION DAYS

EDITOR'S NOTE

In this single volume we have combined two beloved collections of stories by Julie du St. Esprit (1868-1947), a prolific writer whose name appeared on her many works only as "A Sister of Notre Dame." However, a brief note is necessary to explain a slight modification you will find in this edition.

At the time that the original book *True Stories for First Communicants* was published in 1919, a very strict Eucharistic fast was observed, requiring those who wished to receive Communion to be fasting, even from water, from midnight of the previous night. Naturally, this was a difficult restriction, especially for little children. So the first story in this book is about Reggie, a little boy who forgets and has a cup of water on his First Communion day. He bravely accepts the consequences and receives Baby Jesus the next day instead.

When this book came to be reprinted in 1949, the Eucharistic Fast had by then been modified to allow the drinking of water, and thus, in the reprinted edition, the story of Reggie was replaced with the story of David. There is no record of whether this story was written by the original author or not. Regardless, we felt it made the most sense to include both stories in this volume.

Some children—and even adults—may find the story of Reggie somewhat distressing. However, we feel it is a wonderful example of the great love and reverence that even little children have shown throughout history for our Blessed Lord in the Eucharist. Let us take to heart Reggie's courageous faithfulness to that love, even in the face of what we would deem a real hardship, and seek to imitate it in our own lives.

One more brief note we wish to share: the original editions of these two books contained handsome illustrations by Wilfrid Pippet; in the 1949 reprints, these were updated by Rosemary de Souza. We are pleased to have been able to restore the original illustrations in this edition.

In Christ,
Lisa Bergman
St. Augustine Academy Press
Feast of St. Gregory the Great, 2019

TRUE STORIES FOR FIRST COMMUNICANTS

AUTHOR'S NOTE

I t is the writer's wish that these simple stories be put into the hands, not only of those preparing for their First Holy Communion, but also of those little ones who have already had this happiness, so that the example of these other children, some of whom have already received the reward of their virtues, may encourage them to persevere in the love of Our Blessed Lord. For this reason lives have been given of those who have persevered to the end, as well as of those still working out their salvation.

FIRST SUNDAY OF ADVENT, 1918

PREFACE

hese stories are admirable, very direct, most simple and true. They are all about First Communicants, mostly of our own day, and among the poor.

It is clear that the writer knows how to catch and hold the attention of children, and that she can, moreover, write a story exactly as she would tell it—a rarer gift indeed, if it be a gift and not simply literary courage.

The youngest communicant will be able to follow gladly these stories when read aloud, without any editing or explanations; and older children will delight to read them more than once for themselves. The hearts of grownup people will be touched by their tender pathos, and will be moved, likely enough, to tears, by more than one of these spiritual tragedies in infant souls.

By a true instinct, if not of set purpose, the writer has avoided the monstrous perversions of fact and horrible tales of supposed sacrilege with which too often pious people think to frighten the child into reverence. Happily, too, there is nothing here in the way of exaggeration, no flavour of the spiritual fairytale, nothing fantastic nor even imaginative, beyond the imagination that goes with genuine insight and sympathy. No child will need to be told that these tales are true. Their truth is evident in the directness and sincerity of the narrative. They are too objective, too simply told, to be creations of the writer's brain. Children are punctilious regarding the reality and solid truth of matters concerning God, and religion is not helped but rather discredited in their fresh minds by flights of fancy and far-fetched inventions that may yet regale the jaded faculties of certain older people. "But was he a real man?" asked the small boy before he would adopt the saint as an example.

We welcome, then, these stories and commend them, both for what they are, and even more, perhaps, for what they are not. Our hope is that the author may soon give us a second series—all from the everyday life of our own poor children: for these are the kind that give most pleasure and will do most good.

W. ROCHE, S. J.

FEAST OF THE HOLY INNOCENTS, 1918.

REGGIE

A few years ago in a large convent school you might have seen a happy band of children getting ready for their First Holy Communion. Such little mites they looked, nine boys and seven girls, the youngest only six, the eldest eight years old. Though they were so young they were very much in earnest, all trying to fill their hearts with beautiful flowers for Little Baby Jesus. Day after day they would come running in to tell Sister of some fresh flower just added to the rest. It would be: "Sister, I gave a penny to a poor boy coming to school!" or: "Sister, I turned the rope three times instead of jumping," or a fidgety little mite would say: "Sister, I never looked round once the whole lesson," and so on, each wanting Sister to know how much he or she was trying.

The First Communion Day was to be on the 25th of March, the beautiful Feast of the Annunciation. Now all preparations were made. Each little soul had been washed in the Precious

1

Blood of Our Dear Lord in Confession the day before, and the great morning of the 25th had come. Such a beautiful spring morning it was. One by one the children arrived, the little girls in their white dresses with their snowy veils and wreaths of roses on their heads, and the little boys in nice suits. As they came in, each sat quietly in a little chair in class, until all were ready. One little lad, in changing his shoes, had soiled his fingers and asked if he might go and wash them. "I couldn't go to Holy Communion with dirty fingers, could I, Sister?" he said as he went. Alas! how little Sister or he thought what that little act would cost him.

As he was washing his fingers he spied a little cup just beside the basin. Without a thought he filled it to the brim and took a long refreshing drink, then, running quickly back to the others he sat down contentedly in his chair. Two minutes later there was a knock at the door. Sister was wanted. One of the servants was there; she came to say she thought—she wasn't sure, but she thought she had caught sight of one of the little gentlemen taking a drink of water. Sister's heart sank within her. Could it be true? Returning to the children she said quietly, "Did any little boy forget and take a drink of water?"

Poor little Reggie! In an instant it flashed into his mind what he had done. With the remembrance came the temptation not to tell, but it was only for a moment. No, he would be brave. White as his little suit, and trembling from head to foot, he looked up at the Sister. "Oh; Sister, I did—I never thought. Oh, Sister, what can I do?" Tenderly drawing the child to her side Sister tried to comfort him, telling him that he need only wait till tomorrow. But the poor little fellow seemed quite stunned, unable to realise what it all meant.

Then they went up to chapel in procession. Reggie knelt beside Sister. What were his thoughts as he knelt there in that beautiful chapel, watching the priest and listening to the sweet singing? Presently the bell rang for the Elevation. Then the children made aloud their short "Acts before Holy Communion." The longed-for moment had at last arrived. Slowly and reverently the little ones went up to the altar rails—all but Reggie. Only then did the truth really dawn upon him—Baby Jesus could not come into his heart. All would receive Him, only he would be left out. Poor little Reggie, he burst into passionate sobs, startling all in the chapel.

He was obliged to be taken out that the others might not be disturbed.

All that day he joined with the others in their games and amusements. Such a sad little face he had among the others whose hearts were overflowing with peace and happiness.

But the next morning very early, when all his little companions of the day before were still in bed, Reggie's father and mother brought him once more to the convent. No music and singing to be heard today. All the music was in Reggie's heart as at last Baby Jesus entered it for the first time. How much he had to tell Him—all about the long weeks of preparation and then about the bitter disappointment of the day before. But how happy he was now, and how quickly the moments flew. "I had to finish talking to Jesus all the way out of chapel!" he said. But I don't think he or his little companions could ever forget that they must be "fasting from midnight."

DAVID

avid and John lived in the same buildings. Their flats were next to one another aand the two boys were like brothers. Both were Catholics, but both attended a non-Catholic school, for alas, there was no Catholic one anywhere near. But there was a Catholic Church and on Saturdays and Sundays the Catholic children were given special instructions and prepared for Confession and Holy Communion. There were two classes, one for the tinies and one for those rather older.

One day John and David started Sunday School together. John was seven and could nearly read so he was put in the higher class, but David was not yet six and very, very tiny for his age, indeed he looked only about four years old, but he was clever and could read even better than John.

After they had attended some weeks on Sundays, John was told that he could now come on Saturdays as well and begin to prepare for his First Confession and Holy Communion: but David was in the little ones' class.

Saturday came, the children were seated in the Hall with their teacher, when in walked John and David.

"And who is this little mite?" asked the teacher.

"This is David," replied John, "he would come. He wants to make his Confession and Holy Communion too. He says Jesus wants him to come."

"I'm afraid he's too little," replied the teacher, "you see you will have to learn prayers and Catechism and be able to answer the questions the Priest will ask you, and he seems only a baby."

"Oh, he's not a baby, he is almost six and reads better than I do."

"Well, he may stay today, for I suppose he could not go home alone."

All this time David said nothing. He went over to the chairs and sat down beside the other children. All through the lesson he sat listening attentively but did not speak one word. The lesson over he and John went home together.

John had been given two answers to learn and told to be sure to know his *Hail Mary* perfectly by next week.

The next Saturday came and again John and David both walked in and sat down. The teacher looked at David but said nothing. One by one the children stood up, repeated the two answers and said the *Hail Mary*. When the child sitting next to David had said hers, to the teacher's surprise David immediately stood up, said the two answers and the *Hail Mary* perfectly, and sat down again.

Week after week the same thing happened. John and David always knew whatever they had been given to learn; every Sunday they were both at Mass.

One Saturday the Priest came in to see how the children were getting on. He at once caught sight of David. "Who is that baby?" he asked, "what is he doing in the First Communion Class?" The teacher told him how David had persisted in coming with John, his friend, and how well he had learnt his prayers and Catechism.

Sitting down the priest called David to him. He asked him many questions, to all of which David gave good and clear answers.

"Don't you think you are too young to make your first Holy Communion?" he asked.

"No, Father," replied David. "I must make it with John, I'm six now, and Jesus wants me to come."

The Priest smiled and turning to the teacher he said, "He may go on preparing with the others and if he is still anxious to make it there is no reason why he should not; his size does not matter. So now, David, it's all right, you may go on coming with John, but be sure you never miss Sunday Mass." David went back to his place contentedly, smiling at John.

Weeks went by, the time arrived for the children to make their First Confession. The Priest had called to see David's mother. She was not a Catholic, her husband was, but he was away at sea, for he was in the Navy. David's mother was quite ready to allow David to make his First Holy Communion. "He and John have grown up together," she said, "I would not like him to be disappointed, besides I promised my husband David should be brought up a Catholic."

So David made his First Confession with the other children and began with them to prepare for his First Holy Communion. The teacher gave each child a small paper heart on which they could mark down all they did to please Jesus while preparing for His Visit.

Before their Confession, in order to arouse their gratitude to Jesus, she had told them the story of the "Ten Lepers", noting how only one of the ten had returned to give thanks to Jesus. At the same time she reminded them how many, many acts of kindness their fathers and mothers did for them and how very often they never even thanked them or showed in any way that they were grateful. If they were not grateful to their fathers and mothers, they would not be grateful to Jesus.

This story made a great impression on David, he often thought about it, and would say to himself, "I would have been the grateful leper, I would have come back to thank Jesus."

The teacher had also told them two or three times to remember whatever they did or gave up to others for love of Jesus, Jesus would count it as being done for Him, and Jesus was always grateful.

David said nothing, even to John, about this— but he was always on the look-out for something he could do. It was about this time that his mother noticed how quick he was to see anything he could do to help her, eager and ready to run her messages, to help her wash up the dishes after meals, to shell the peas, or even peel the potatoes; but what gave David the most delight was to give his mother surprises. One day she would find on her plate an ice-cream or some sweets bought with David's pocket money, another time it would be some flowers or a pretty ornament he had seen in some shop window. When mother did something for him he would give her a hug and never forget to thank her. All these little Acts would be marked down on his paper heart to give to Jesus on his First Communion Day.

At last the great day of the First Communion arrived. David's mother came with John's mother to the Mass, she had never been present at a First Communion before. The little girls were all dressed in white frocks, white veils and white wreaths. The little boys wore their best suits with long white armlets and rosettes on the lapels of their coats.

As the children entered she noticed that her own little son was leading the procession—so tiny he looked, yet so serious, as with hands joined and eyes lowered he led the way to the front bench.

When she saw all those little children approach the altar rails to receive their Jesus and watched them return so reverently to their places her heart was touched and the tears came into her eyes. What a wonderful religion the Catholic one must be where even little children could pray so well! She thought of all the little acts of kindness she had received from David whilst he had been preparing for this great day, and she determined she would find out if it were possible for her to become a Catholic too.

David did not give up trying as some children do when the first great day is over, which is very ungrateful to Jesus. "I am always going to be the grateful leper," he said to himself. He used to make himself little paper hearts, and each week he had quite a number of kind acts to write down, for each Sunday he went to Holy Communion. "I mustn't disappoint Jesus," he told his mother, "He wants me to come."

Not only did he go to Holy Communion himself each Sunday, but he persuaded John to come too. Sometimes John wanted to play with the other boys or go to the Pictures on a Saturday morning instead of going to Confession; but David would go up to him saying, "Come on, John, you know mother doesn't like me going alone, and I do so want to go." And John, who was very fond of David, would give up what he was doing and go with him to Confession.

So the two little boys faithfully kept to their weekly Communion for a whole year, then David's father came home. He was very pleased to hear all about the First Communion and promised to go with David the following Sunday. But to John's grief, very soon after that David and his father and mother went to live in another part of England. Here they were near a Catholic school which David was able to attend. But John never forgot his little friend and still kept up his weekly Communion, which so pleased the priest that he allowed John to serve on the altar, which is a great privilege.

ST. GERARD MAJELLA

ou have all heard of the wonderful saint called St. Gerard Majella, how he spent his whole life doing good, curing those who were ill, making wicked men feel sorry for their sins, and become good again, loving Our Dear Lord in the tabernacle so much, and being loved so much by Him that whatever he prayed for was granted.

Now St. Gerard was once a little boy just like one of you, only he was an Italian boy. He was born in a pretty little town in Italy called Muro. His father kept a tailor's shop and used to make clothes for the men who lived there. He was a good man and loved God, and wished his children to grow up good Catholics. God had given him three children, two girls and one little boy, Gerard, the youngest. The very day he was born his father carried him to the Cathedral and had him baptized so that he might at once become a child of God. His mother, who loved her son very much, took great care of him, and as soon as he could speak, taught him to say the Holy Names of Jesus and Mary. His mother noticed that whenever she talked to his sisters of God and His Holy Mother, Gerard would leave his play and come and sit quietly at her side. When they said their prayers Gerard would join his little hands and his lips moved as if he were trying to say the words.

One day, when Gerard was three or four years old, he heard his mother explaining to his sisters how Jesus dwelt in the tabernacle in church, and how often He was left alone hour after hour, and yet never wearied of waiting for us there. This was enough for Gerard. Quietly he slipped out of the room; out of the front door, and trotted down the street to the church. The door was open, so in he went, right up the middle, up to the top of the altar steps. There he knelt, talking to Jesus, his little hands clasped, his eyes fixed on the tabernacle door. Two hours passed and still he knelt on. People coming in and out wondered to see that tiny child kneeling there, but no one disturbed him.

Meanwhile father and mother and friends were all looking for Gerard. Gerard was lost! Where could he be? His mother at last went into the church to ask the help of Our Lady who once lost her dear Son for three days. Imagine her surprise when, on going into the church, she saw her lost baby rapt in prayer on the altar steps.

With a cry of joy she hastened to him, lifted him in her arms and carried him home. "Where have you been, Gerard, all this time?" she asked.

"Only in church, mamma," he said. "I did not want Little Jesus to be lonely."

After this Gerard would slip away from home day after day, but he could always be found just in front of the altar, talking to Jesus. Never was he so happy as when he was talking to Our Blessed Lord in church.

One day he came home with a tiny loaf which he gave to his mother. When she asked him where he had got it he told her that the lovely lady in the church had given it to him. This happened several times. His sister Bridget, curious to see who took such notice of her little brother, one day followed him at a distance. Imagine her surprise to see Gerard stop in front of the beautiful statue of Our Lady with the Infant Jesus, and looking up, say: "Come down, Little One. Here I am." Before Gerard had time to say any more a wonderful thing happened. The Holy Child was standing beside him and when his sister looked again at the statue, Our Lady's arms were empty. Jesus kissed and talked to little Gerard, then, giving him a little white loaf, He once more returned to His Blessed Mother's arms.

Quickly Bridget ran home to tell her mother the wonderful miracle she had seen, and the good mother thanked God for having given her a son who was so pleasing to God as to be allowed to play with the Infant Jesus.

As Gerard grew a little older he began to have a great desire to receive his dear Jesus in Holy Communion. He had seen his eldest sister make her First Holy Communion when she was twelve years old, for in those days it was not the custom for very little children to receive Our Lord. They had to wait until they were twelve or thirteen years old, and Gerard was not seven. Many a time he asked his mother to let him go, but she only smiled and told him to wait a little longer.

But one day during Holy Mass, as Gerard watched the people going up to the communion rails, he felt he could not wait another moment.

Jesus seemed to be calling him. Joining his hands reverently he walked up to the rails and knelt between two ladies. The priest came down from the altar with Our Lord in his hands. He went to the end of the rails and began giving Holy Communion to each one there. Nearer and nearer he came to where Gerard was kneeling; only two more, only one, and he stands in front of Gerard, whose heart beat so violently he could hardly breathe. But the priest looked at the little one, then thinking it some baby who had crept up with its mother, passed him by, gave Holy Communion to the other lady and then returned to the altar. Gerard, opening his eyes, saw Our Lord had passed him by. With one big sob he rose, left the church, and hastened home. Once in his own little room he threw himself on the ground and sobbed as if his little heart would break.

His mother heard all about what had happened from a neighbour who had been there, and when much later Gerard came down, his eyes swollen with crying, she asked no questions but, kissing him tenderly, tried to amuse him and make him think of something else.

At half-past six that night, after his mother had left him safely tucked up in bed and gone downstairs, Gerard began once more to cry quietly to himself. Then a wonderful thing happened. He could see the sky from where he lay, and he seemed to see right up into heaven, the home of Little Jesus. Presently, as he lay gazing up and praying for the great grace for which he longed, he saw the heavens open, and the beautiful archangel St. Michael come flying down towards him, carrying in his hands the Sacred Host. In an instant Gerard was on his knees. St. Michael flew right to Gerard, and placed on the tongue of the happy child his dear Jesus.

And so, from the hands of the great Saint Michael himself, Gerard received his First Holy Communion.

KITTY

itty was not a pretty little girl, nor did she wear grand clothes, nor was she a Catholic, but her father and mother thought her nearly perfect and loved her dearly. Little Jesus did not think her perfect, but He loved her much more even than her father and mother, and so He chose her out to be one of His own little lambs, and took her little soul to heaven before it had ever been spoiled by any big sin.

I told you how dearly her father and mother loved her. Now, at this time, when Kitty was five years old, they were very troubled because she was not happy at school; every day there were tears because teacher had been cross with her. At last mother took her to a Catholic school and asked them to take her in there. When the Sister hesitated because Kitty was not a Catholic, her mother begged Sister to take her because she had always heard children were so happy at Catholic schools. At last the Sister consented, and the following week Kitty went to the convent just as if she had been a little Catholic girl.

Now it was quite a different tale. As soon as she woke in the morning she said: "Mother, isn't it time to get up? Mother, don't let me be late for school, the first lesson is best of all." The first lesson was Catechism, and Kitty loved it. Such wonderful stories about Almighty God, Our Lord and His Blessed Mother and the Saints, all true stories too. One day Kitty came home full of excitement. Some of the little ones had made their First Holy Communion that morning, and Kitty had seen them in their white veils and wreaths. She had asked why they were dressed like that, and had been told that that morning Little Jesus had come into their hearts for the first time. Now some of them were not much older than Kitty herself, so the little girl said nothing but waited.

Not long afterwards Kitty had her sixth birthday and felt quite a big girl. As soon as she arrived at school she went up to Sister and said "Please, Sister, I am six years old to-day; and Mary is only six and a half."

Mary was one of the little girls who had lately made her First Holy Communion.

"Well, Kitty," said the Sister, as she gave her a birthday kiss, "I hope you will have a very happy birthday. So now you have nearly caught up Mary, is that what you want to do?"

"Yes, Sister. May I have Little Jesus in my heart today? Mary did."

"But Mary is a Catholic, dear, and only little Catholic girls may make their First Holy Communion."

"Then please make me a Catholic, Sister."

"I can't do that, dear. You must ask father and mother about it."

Sister sighed, and Kitty went to her place and did her lessons, but from that day the tears began again at home. She kept saying "Oh, mother dear, I do want to be a Catholic. Won't you let me be a Catholic?"

"Nonsense, Kitty," her mother would say. "Isn't your father's religion good enough for you?"

"No, mother: I can't have Little Jesus unless I'm a Catholic."

But her mother did not understand what the child was talking about.

Then Kitty would try her father. "Daddy dear, wouldn't you like to make me very happy?"

"Yes, dear, if I can. What do you want?"

"Oh, Daddy, do let me be a Catholic. I do want Little Jesus. Oh, Daddy dear, do."

But her daddy did not understand either.

This went on so often that at last her mother said she would try another school where they didn't put such funny ideas into children's heads. This frightened Kitty so much that she promised she would never ask to be a Catholic again if they would only leave her where she was. So for a time there was peace once more at home. Several months went by, and again at school a happy group of children made their First Holy Communion. Poor little Kitty, she had been so sure Little Jesus would have come to her this year. Many a time now she cried herself to sleep.

Soon her mother thought she was looking pale and thin and took her to the doctor.

"The child is fretting," said the doctor. "Do you know what it is about?"

"It's all because of that school she is at," said her mother.

"Then you had better change her school," said the doctor. "She'll never get better if she goes on fretting."

That evening her mother and father talked it over. If they took her away from the school she would fret, and if they left her there as she was she would fret.

Why not let her be a Catholic? It seemed as good a religion as their own and even better.

So the next day father and mother went to the school and arranged with Sister to have Kitty received into the Catholic Church. They promised to do all in their power to help her to practise her religion. Then they went home, and her father, taking Kitty on his knee, told her what they had done. Kitty could not thank her parents enough. She seemed quite a changed little girl altogether.

Now she would tell father and mother all the beautiful stories of Little Jesus that she heard at her school; and when it came to making her First Confession she told them all about it, and how dear Jesus was going to wash her soul so beautifully white. Wouldn't they like their souls washed too, she asked. But neither father nor mother knew how to answer her.

Kitty made her First Confession, and soon after began to prepare for her First Holy Communion. So hard did she try to be good, and so often did she give up little things for her dear Jesus, that her mother was quite puzzled.

"I can't understand the child at all," she said. "Kitty used to be so fond of sweets. Now she's always giving them away; and as for cakes and jam, she hardly touches them. Yet I've never known her so happy and contented."

At last came her First Communion day. What a day of bliss!

"I feel too happy to live," said Kitty to her mother that night. "How lovely it would be to die and always live with Little Jesus."

"Would you leave father and me all alone?" said her mother.

"I could see you all the time if I were up in heaven," said Kitty, "and I would ask Little Jesus to let you come too."

When a little later Kitty received the Holy Sacrament of Confirmation she took the name of Mary Imelda, because, she said, "Little Jesus took Imelda to live with Him always after her First Holy Communion."

Then as the months slipped by Kitty would go to Holy Communion as often as her mother would let her. She grew brighter and happier every day, and was like a ray of sunshine in the house.

"How glad I am she is a Catholic!" said her daddy. "It makes me feel better to look at her."

"Yes," said her mother, "and when she says her prayers night and morning she looks just like a little angel."

Little Jesus too liked to look at Kitty. He had been helping her to make her soul more and more beautiful, till now it was like a lovely lily just opening. "This lily must never become soiled or faded;" said Little Jesus. "I will take it up to heaven and plant it in my garden where it will never fade."

So one day He sent Kitty an illness called diphtheria. She was so ill that the doctor took her to the hospital. Everybody was very kind to her there. One day a dear old priest went to see her. He told her that Little Jesus wanted her to live with Him in heaven.

"Oh, I am so glad," said Kitty, and when her father and mother came to see her she told them the good news, adding: "And I will ask Little Jesus to let you come too."

But her mother and father were very sad, for they knew how lonely they would be without their little girl.

The next day Kitty fell asleep, and when she awoke where do you think she was? Right up in heaven with Little Jesus, happy for evermore. She did not forget her father and mother.

The next year her father died too, but before he died he sent for a priest and asked him to let him die a Catholic like his little Kitty. The priest instructed and baptized him, and soon after he went to heaven to meet his little girl. Then only the mother was left and she asked the priest to baptize her too. "For," said she, "I must be with Kitty and daddy when my turn comes."

MARIE

This story happened about fifty years ago, when there was a war between Germany and France in 1870. The Germans had brought their large armies into France, and many battles were fought there.

One night when the Germans were near a village called Dijon, they sent scouts on to say that their soldiers would rest in that village for the night, and would sleep in the church, which was the only large building there.

When the people of the village heard this they were in great distress. The priest was not at home and many of these soldiers were wicked men; and it would not have been right to leave Our Lord in the tabernacle of the church where the soldiers might insult Him. Yet they could not prevent the German soldiers from doing what they said they would do.

Now you know that no one but a priest or deacon should take the Blessed Sacrament in his hands except in cases of necessity. No one should touch the ciborium or sacred vessel in which It is kept without special permission. But when soldiers were going to sleep in the church it was of course "a case of necessity." Yet not one of the villagers dared to take the ciborium away. First they asked the sacristan who cleaned the church, but he said "No." Then they asked one man after the other, but each was afraid; or said he was not worthy. What was to be done? Soon it would be too late.

At last one of the men said: "I know what to do. My little daughter Marie is four years old. She is good and innocent, just like an angel. I will take her up to the altar. She shall take Our Lord from the tabernacle, and then we will carry her to the priest's house, while she holds the ciborium in her baby hands."

All were very pleased with this idea. So Marie was sought for. Her mother washed her, especially her little hands that were so soon to carry Our Dear Lord, and dressed her in her best white frock, while she tried to explain to her the great honour she was to have.

Marie seemed to understand quite well. Since she was a tiny baby her mother had taken her to visit Little Jesus in the tabernacle, and many a time she had blown Him kisses from the church door. Now she was to carry Him in her arms.

Slowly and reverently her father carried her up the altar steps, and unlocked the tabernacle door. Lovingly Marie drew out the ciborium which held her dear Jesus and pressed it to her breast. Her little heart beat fast while she whispered to Jesus how pleased she was to have Him in her arms. Tighter and tighter she clasped the white silk veil which covered Our Lord's little golden house. Tighter and tighter her father held his little girl in his arms, for was she not bearing in her tiny hands the Lord and God who bears us all in the hollow of His Hand, and yet loves us so much that He hides Himself in the Blessed Sacrament just to be always with us when we need Him?

After Marie's father walked all the villagers, making quite a long procession, until they came to the priest's house. There Our Lord remained safely all night, the good villagers taking it in turns to kneel on guard in front of Him.

Now you will want to know why Marie was chosen instead of one of the men for this great honour. It was because she was so innocent and

Tighter and tighter her Father held his little girl

pure: she had never committed any sin and so had never offended dear Jesus. It is into pure and innocent hearts like hers that Jesus loves to come in Holy Communion.

Very soon, when the priest came back, the villagers told him all that they had done, and he was very pleased, and told Marie that she must always remember what a great honour she had had, and that she must begin to prepare her heart to become a home for the same dear Jesus whom she had carried in her hands.

JOHN

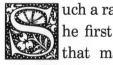uch a ragged, dirty little boy he was when he first came to school, and so naughty that many a time his teacher was in despair over him.

But it was no wonder John was naughty. He had never been taught to be anything else. His father and mother were tramps who spent all their lives going from one village to another begging; then when they got a few pence they spent them at the nearest public-house. They never spoke without swearing and using bad language, which John thought very clever. From a tiny child he had tried to copy them in every way, until he, too, never spoke without using bad language.

He was always in rags, and had never known what it was to wear shoes and stockings, nor could he ever remember staying longer than a week at any place until he was about eight years of age. At that time they were near Manchester, when John's mother fell ill, so they went to live in a tiny room in one of the worst streets in that city.

Now it happened, that John's mother was a Catholic, though not a good one. She had never been inside a church since she was a little girl at school, but feeling herself so ill she thought about the bad life she had led, and how John had never been baptized. So one day when his father was out she sent John to look for a priest. John went out into the street, asked someone to tell him where a priest could be found, and soon returned with him to his mother.

The priest stayed a long time with her, for he saw she was dying, and he wanted to help her to be sorry for the bad life she had led. He promised, too, that John should be baptized and put into a Catholic school. Soon after this his mother died, but not before the priest had done all he could for her and for John, and John's father made up his mind to stay in Manchester now his wife was dead.

John did not like school at all. He had spent the whole of his life roaming about the country, and he could not see why he should be made to sit still and learn all sorts of things he did not want to know. So he behaved as badly as he could, and did his best to make the others naughty too. The only time that John was good in school was during religious instruction. He had never heard the life of Our Lord before, and when he first heard the story of the Passion he cried bitterly. If his teacher had not noticed this, I think she would have had him sent away from the school, but she thought she would get him to be good for the love of Our Lord.

One day she asked him to walk home with her so that she might talk to him alone. She explained to him how he hurt Our Lord by his bad behaviour, and by the bad language he used. John replied that he did not want to be naughty but that he never thought, and that he did not know when he was using bad language. He just spoke the same way as his father. His teacher said she would give him a little picture of the Sacred Heart and told him when in school to keep it on his desk to remind him, and John promised that he would try to do better.

Each morning he took out his picture as his teacher had told him, and many a time, just as he was going to begin some trick to make the boys laugh, his eyes fell upon it and he went on with his lessons instead. He did not get good all at once though: many and many a time he had to be punished. But he went on trying, and that was what his teacher wanted.

The next year he made his First Confession. His great trouble was his habit of swearing. It seemed as if he could not cure himself. You see he had always heard this language from his father when at home. The following year the priest put him in the First Communion class, but told him he really must overcome this habit if he wished to receive Our Lord with the other children.

John often tried to do little acts to please Our Lord, and it made him sad to think he had so little to give Him. One day his teacher asked the children instead of buying sweets to bring their money for some very poor children, and in this way to show their love for Our Lord. Poor John was very sad about this. What could he give? He had nothing at all. The next day, to his joy, his father gave him a halfpenny to buy his dinner. John was delighted. He ran all the way to school, and handing his halfpenny to the teacher, asked her to take one farthing for the poor and the change would do for his dinner. Do you not think Our Lord must have loved him?

A month later, on the Feast of Corpus Christi, the children were to make their First Holy Communion. Although John still used bad words sometimes, he was so much better that the priest said he might make it too. The day before, John went to Confession, and was glad to think there was only the night to pass before Our Lord would come to him. He had no nice clothes to wear, nothing but his rags, but his teacher had told him to wash himself well and she would lend him a coat, as he had not got one. So when it was time to go to bed he got some water and began to wash himself vigorously. His father asked him what he was doing that for, and John told him. He had only once or twice before spoken to his father about religion, for each time it had made him so angry that he had beaten John cruelly, so the boy thought it wiser to say nothing about it. But that night he had answered without thinking.

When his father heard what John was going to do the next day he was so angry that he began using the most dreadful language, and took up a stick to beat him.

"Oh, father, beat me if you will," said John, as he put his hands to his ears, "but do not use such dreadful words. I cannot stay here if you do."

"So your own father's language is not good enough for you! And you can't stay here? You shall not stay here. Go and find a home for yourself." And pushing him out of the door the angry man shut it, and left his little boy in the street.

It was dark. John walked slowly down the street until he found a doorstep where he would be nearly hidden if a policeman passed. Then, sitting down, he took out his rosary and quietly said his prayers till he fell asleep.

Early in the morning he awoke stiff and cold. But he did not think of that. He only remembered it was his First Communion day and ran off towards his school.

His teacher was there with the other First Communicants, and lent him the coat she had promised, pinning a white ribbon on to the sleeve. How happy John was as he walked up to the communion rails with the others, and it was only after the breakfast at the school, when John was talking to the priest, that he told him where he had spent the night.

"You see, Father," he said, "I was so afraid if I listened to those dreadful words I should be repeating them to myself without thinking, and so stain my soul."

So, in order to make a pure home for Our Lord in his heart, John had lost his earthly home. But you will be pleased to hear that the priest found a new, good Catholic home for him, where he grew up to become a good and useful man.

LITTLE NELLIE

This is a story of a little girl called Nellie—such a little girl that she was not much more than a baby when her beautiful guardian angel took her soul up to heaven. Yet this little baby had learnt to love "Holy God" more than many children who were much older than she.

When Nellie was only three years old her dear mamma died, and there was no one to take care of the home and the children, for Nellie's father was a soldier and had to live with the other soldiers. So little Nellie and her sister were sent to live in a convent school kept by the kind Good Shepherd Sisters. When the two little girls arrived at the convent it was found that Nellie had the whooping cough, so she was taken right away to the hospital for some weeks. After she was better she came back to the convent and lived with the other little children. All the others were much bigger than Nellie, and they were very pleased to have a dear little baby girl to play with. They made a great pet of her, and did all they could to make her happy.

Yet, in spite of all their kindness, Nellie was often found crying. She cried so often, for nothing as people thought, that they said she must be a very bad-tempered little girl. But this was not really so.

After a few weeks Nellie became very ill, and they found that every time she had cried she had been suffering great pain, but was too tiny to explain what was the matter with her. Now she was ill, too ill to stay with the other children, so ill indeed that they thought she was going to die. So she was carried to a dear little cottage at the end of the convent garden, where sick children were nursed.

One of the big girls used to take care of her when the Sister was busy. Nearly every day this big girl used to get up early to go to Mass and Holy Communion in the convent chapel, but sometimes when she was not very well she was told to stay in bed instead.

The first morning this happened, when she got up and came into Nellie's room, Nellie looked up from her cot and said: "You haven't had Holy God in your heart today."

"How do you know that, Nellie?" asked the big girl.

"Oh, I know," said Nellie, "and I shall tell Mother."

(The children call the Sisters "Mother" in that convent.)

Every time that the big girl stayed in bed Nellie knew; although she was not sleeping in the same room. Each time that she came in Nellie would look at her sadly and say:

"You have not had Holy God today."

The Sister who looked after Nellie used to teach her all about Almighty God, and His Dear Mother, and how to say her little prayers.

Nellie loved to hear about "Holy God" (as she said), and about Holy God's Mother and the angels.

One day during Exposition of the Blessed Sacrament, Sister carried Nellie into the chapel and told her all about Holy God living there. After this Nellie seemed to think of nothing else. She understood all about Holy Communion too, and would ask the Sister who nursed her to come straight up to her bed after she had received Our Lord, while Holy God was still in her heart.

The Bishop, when he heard about little Nellie and her great love for Holy God, said he would come to the convent and give her the holy Sacrament of

Confirmation. So one day the Bishop came, and Sister carried little Nellie into the chapel, for she was too weak to walk, and there, as she lay in the Sister's arms, the good Bishop confirmed her. After this Nellie longed to make her First Holy Communion. "When will Holy God come into my heart?" she would ask. "Oh, I am longing for Holy God."

About this time there was a good priest staying in the convent. He often used to visit little Nellie, and when he found how ardently she longed for Holy God, and how well she understood about Holy Communion, he said she should be allowed to make her First Communion. The Bishop's permission was asked and given. Then little Nellie was told that soon indeed Holy God was to come into her heart. How happy she was as she lay in her tiny cot watching the preparations!

Near her cot they had made a little altar to the Infant Jesus, and Nellie would lie for hours looking at it and talking to Holy God. They made her a little white frock, a white veil and wreath, and lent her little white shoes and socks to wear. Nellie took a great interest in these clothes.

"Everything must be very nice for Holy God," she said, "and you must put them on me again when He takes me up to heaven."

The morning came, and Nellie was dressed and carried into chapel, and there they laid her on a cushion on one of the benches. All the Sisters were there and all the children too. The children sang very sweetly during the Mass, but Nellie clasped her tiny hands and said her baby prayers. When at last the priest brought her Holy Communion, how happy she was! Dear little baby, sitting there so quietly, talking to Holy God! After her thanksgiving she was carried out of the chapel back to her cot. Such a happy, contented little baby had never been known before.

Her next Holy Communion was during the Christmas Midnight Mass. After that she grew worse and worse. The priest used to bring Holy God to her in bed. Such a brave little girl she was, although she suffered most terrible pain. She would say: "Look at Holy God on the Cross. He suffered more than this for me. Oh, I am longing to go to Holy God."

But her time was growing very short on earth now. Each day she grew weaker and weaker, until one Sunday a beautiful angel flew down from heaven for Nellie's soul and took it up with him to Holy God. The Sisters and children were very sorry to lose their baby playmate, and all were present when Nellie's poor little body was put into a tiny grave in the convent grounds. Afterward they often went to pray where Nellie was buried, and from her place in heaven little Nellie helped them by her prayers. The memory of her great love for Holy God made them try to love Him too as she did, and to take great pains to prepare their hearts to receive Him in Holy Communion.

TARCISIUS

Long, long ago the Romans were the most famous and most powerful people in the world. In their great city of Rome the Christians were often very cruelly treated, just because they loved and honoured Jesus Christ. Often they were thrown into dark and dirty prisons, from which they were only taken in order to be martyred. Sometimes Christians were beaten or burnt to death. Sometimes they were thrown to lions or panthers in a large open space surrounded by rows of seats, called the Coliseum. To keep out of the way of the pagan Romans, so that they might live in safety, the Christians dug deep down into the earth and made long passages and rooms. The openings to these hiding-places were made in lonely spots outside the city, and only the Christians knew where they were.

These underground places were called "catacombs," and Holy Mass was said there, and there the Christians used to receive Holy Communion and have instructions from the bishops and priests.

But in spite of all the care that was taken to keep everything secret, the pagans sometimes found the openings into the catacombs, and then the Christians were caught and put in prison or condemned to death. At the time that this story happened a great many Christians had been caught and were in prison expecting every day to be put to death. These brave soldiers of Christ sent a message to the Bishop asking him to send them Holy Communion, for they knew that just as food makes our bodies strong, so Holy Communion strengthens our souls, and they felt that if they could only receive Our Dear Lord, "the Bread of the strong," into their hearts they would be able to bear any pain or torture for love of Him.

This message reached the Bishop just as he was about to say Mass in one of the catacombs. The underground chapel was quite dark except for the candles on the altar, but all who were kneeling there could see the Bishop as he turned round before he began his Mass and asked all present to pray that he might choose the best messenger to carry the Blessed Sacrament to the prisoners. No priest could do this, because he would be at once seized and imprisoned, and most of the other Christians were well known too.

When the Mass was over the Bishop turned round again and asked who would be willing to risk his life to carry Holy Communion to the prisoners. Two or three men offered, but the Bishop was afraid they would be caught and put to death. Then a little boy named Tarcisius came up to the Bishop, and kneeling at his feet begged to be allowed to carry Our Lord to those who needed Him so much.

"I am so young," he said, "the pagans will think I am only a messenger boy, and let me pass."

Tarcisius was an orphan, and well known to all the Christians for his great love of the Blessed Sacrament. At first the Bishop thought he was too young, but Tarcisius begged so hard to be allowed to go that the Bishop at last said "Yes."

Several Sacred Hosts were placed inside a white linen cloth within a little case which Tarcisius put inside his tunic, just over his heart, and with his two hands clasped over his Sacred Burden, he started off.

Oh, how happy and proud Tarcisius felt as he carried Our Blessed Lord so close to his heart! He had no thoughts to spare for places or people that he passed. He thought only of Jesus, Whom he carried.

"Oh, dear Jesus, how I love You!" he whispered. "How good You are to choose me as Your little messenger! How willingly I would suffer and die for You, like these good people in prison! Perhaps one day You will let me lay down my life for you too."

Whispering words of love like these he sped quickly on his way.

He was out of the catacombs now and on the high road. There he passed a group of his school comrades just about to start a game, but needing one more to complete the number. Catching sight of Tarcisius they called to him to stop and join them.

"I am sorry," he said, "but I am on an important message."

He hurried on, but the lads caught hold of him and would not let him go.

"What have you there?" said one, seeing how tightly Tarcisius held his hands to his breast. "Let me see."

"No, no," cried Tarcisius, struggling to free himself.

His anxiety made them all curious, and together they tried to pull away his hands.

"My Jesus, strengthen me," whispered Tarcisius almost under his breath.

But one boy heard the words and cried out to

the others: "He is a Christian. He is hiding some Christian mystery there."

This made the boys still more curious. They determined to see for themselves, so they struck him and kicked him and did their best to pull away his hands, but they could not move them.

A man passing by asked what was the matter. "He's a Christian, carrying some Christian mystery, and we're trying to get it from him," cried one of the boys.

"A Christian did you say?" said the man, and giving Tarcisius one cruel blow, threw him to the ground.

At this very moment a soldier, hastening towards the group, scattered them to right and left and, stooping down, lifted Tarcisius in his arms.

"You cowards!" he said; "all setting on one little lad," and he strode quickly down the street and hurried off into a quiet lane.

"Tarcisius, lad," he said, smoothing back the curls from his pale face.

Tarcisius opened his eyes and recognised the soldier as a Christian whom he had often met in the catacombs.

"I am dying," he said, "but I have kept my God safe from them." And he handed his Precious

"You cowards! All setting on one little lad"

Treasure to the soldier, who placed It reverently inside his tunic. "Carry Him to the prison for me," said Tarcisius, and with a gentle sigh he fell back into the soldier's arms. His little soul was already with God, for whom he so willingly had given his life, for Jesus Himself once said: "Greater love than this no man has, than that a man lay down his life for his friend." Little Tarcisius gave his life for the Friend of friends, Jesus Christ.

JOAN

One night in a small London house a little baby girl was born—such a dear wee baby, with tiny ears like little pink shells, rosy cheeks and a pretty little mouth. But, alas! Something was missing. This little baby had been born with only one eye. On one side of the face a pretty blue eye with long black lashes, and on the other side the eyelashes and the place for the eye, but no eye.

When the mother saw her baby girl, whom she called Joan, she wept, but the father tried to comfort her and said they would take her to a doctor and see what could be done. So baby was taken first to one doctor and then to another, and each tried his skill upon the child, but no doctor could make a real eye grow. You know only Almighty God can do that. Clever men tried their best, and meanwhile the baby was growing bigger and stronger every day. When Joan could walk, and her mother took her out, other children would stand and look at her, and some rude boys even called after her. This made the poor little one very sad, and she would hide her face in her mother's skirts and beg to be left indoors. So her mother bought her a shade, to wear over the place where the other eye should have been. After that people did not notice her so much.

When she was five years old Joan went to school, and as she was a little Catholic girl she went to a school kept by some good Sisters. Her mother told the Sisters all about the missing eye, and asked that her little one might always be allowed to wear her shade. Of course the Sister said that she might, and she also took care that none of the other children should tease her about it. When Joan had been at school a short time she began to lose her fear of others, and would play merrily with her little companions. From time to time she was taken to the doctor, but he said there was now no hope of doing anything for her.

When Joan had been two years at school Sister thought it time for her to prepare for her First Holy Communion, so she and several of her little companions began to attend the special instructions. From the very first the Sister noticed that Joan was one of the most attentive and most in earnest.

Though she did not ask many questions, as some of the others did, not a word was said that she did not remember. What struck Joan most was that it was the Great God Himself who was to come into her heart, God who was all-powerful, and had done such wonderful things when He had lived on earth. Doctors might be clever, but they were not like Almighty God. Ah! she knew what she would ask for on her First Communion day.

Joan's mother was not rich, but she had made a white frock and white veil for her little girl on her First Communion day. "Poor little mite," sighed her mother, as she sewed; "she shall have all I can give her to make her happy."

The First Communion morning arrived. Mother called her little one and began to dress her. When she arranged her hair she was preparing to replace the shade, but Joan stopped her.

"Not this morning, Mother. I would rather not wear it for my First Communion."

"Not wear it?" said her mother, looking at her in surprise, for Joan could hardly bear to be without it even while she dressed.

"You see Jesus is God, and He can do all things,

and I want Him to see me just as I am," answered Joan, and nothing would make her change her resolution.

Very fervently Joan made her First Holy Communion. Many noticed how well she prayed, and how much in earnest she seemed. When she went to breakfast she replaced her shade, which she had brought with her; very few had noticed that she had not worn it the whole time.

The next day the Easter holidays commenced, and her mother took her away for a fortnight, after which she returned to school. The first morning that she was back the Sister sent for her out of the class. Imagine her surprise when Joan came tripping towards her, with no shade on, but two shining eyes smiling up at her instead.

"Why, Joan dear," said Sister, "I am pleased to see that you are cured. So mother has taken you to a very clever doctor during the holidays?"

"Oh no, Sister. It was Holy Communion that cured me," replied Joan simply, "You told us Jesus would give us anything that we asked for on that day, because He was God, so I asked Him to give me my other eye, and it began to grow that day, and now it is just like the other. I have been to Holy Communion every day that I could since."

The Sister could hardly believe that what the child said was true, but Joan's mother came for her that day, and she told the Sister that it had happened just as her little daughter had said.

MARIANA

In the sunny land of Italy lived a little girl called Mariana. Her mother was a rich Countess, the cousin of St. Aloysius Gonzaga, so Mariana was related to a saint. Counting both brothers and sisters the family was eleven in all, and they lived in a beautiful house and had many servants to wait upon them. Only one of Mariana's sisters was married, all the rest were nuns. The Countess was very good and holy, and had taught all her children herself.

Mariana learnt her prayers and catechism as soon as she could talk. Often her mother would take her to church and tell her all about Jesus dwelling in the tabernacle day and night. She showed her the red lamp always burning to tell whoever came into the church that Jesus was there. It made Mariana very happy to know that she could always find Our Lord in church, and that He came into the hearts of those who received Him in Holy Communion.

Although at this time she was only four years old the little girl longed to receive Our Lord into her heart, and she loved kneeling before the tabernacle while she talked to Him. At home she was never so happy as when talking about her dear Jesus, or picking flowers for her little altars.

Sometimes her nurse told her about the sufferings of Our Lord in His Sacred Passion, and of how the saints used to fast and do hard penances in order to be more like Him. Mariana talked all this over with one of her brothers, and they made up their minds to leave home and go and live alone like the saints, spending their time in prayer and penance. So, like another St. Teresa and her brother, they packed up some bread and wine, found where the key of the front door was kept, and then went to bed, meaning to start very early the next morning before anyone was up. But, alas! for their plans. The next morning the basket was found by the servants while Mariana and her little brother were still fast asleep!

When Mariana was eight years old she became very ill, so ill that the doctors thought that she would die. A holy priest came to stay with the Countess, and he told her to pray very fervently to Our Lady Immaculate that Mariana might get better. Mariana said the prayers as her mother told her to do. Then looking up she saw Our Blessed Lady asking Jesus to cure her. It did not seem at first as if Our Lord was going to grant His Mother this favour, but Our Lady went on asking, and at last Jesus said "Yes," and Mariana suddenly felt quite well. She was cured.

You would think that after this great favour Mariana would have tried more than ever to be good, but, strange to say, soon after her cure, instead of trying to please dear Jesus and His Blessed Mother she began to spend her time looking at herself in the glass, curling her hair and thinking how pretty she looked. She even became jealous and cross if her dresses were not as costly and beautiful as those of her friends. She did not do any big sins, but she did not love Our Lord as she had done before. This grieved Jesus very much, for He never left off loving Mariana. So at last He did something to remind the thoughtless little girl of His love.

One day as she was sitting in front of her glass Mariana was thinking what a beautiful face she had, when suddenly, instead of her own face, she saw the face of Our Lord in the mirror. His Sacred Head was crowned with thorns, and

She saw the Face of Our Lord...
His Sacred Head was crowned with Thorns

drops of His Precious Blood were trickling down His cheeks. When Mariana saw this she began to weep, for she knew that her vanity had helped to make Jesus suffer and caused Him to look so sad. There and then she made up her mind that she would never be vain or cross again. She told Our Lord how sorry she was for causing Him pain, and promised to spend more time with Him again.

Mariana kept her promise. Once more she found delight in kneeling before Jesus in the tabernacle, once more she longed to receive Him into her heart in Holy Communion. But she was only eight years old, and in those days it was not the custom to let such little children make their First Holy Communion. Whenever she went to Confession Mariana would ask the priest to let her receive her dear Jesus, but each time he said: "Not yet."

At last, one day in August, the Feast of Our Lady of the Snow, Mariana felt a great desire to go to a certain church built in honour of St. Roch. The Countess gave her permission, and the little girl set off with one of her brothers.

When they arrived at the church numbers of people were already going up to the altar rails to receive Holy Communion. Mariana knelt down near one of the confessionals, and as she watched the people coming back to their places with her dear Jesus in their hearts she began to cry because she could not have Him too. The priest who was hearing confessions noticed this, and called Mariana, asking her to tell him what troubled her. In a voice choked with sobs the little girl told him that it was because she was not yet allowed to make her First Holy Communion, although she wished so much to receive Our Lord.

"But why not, my little friend?" said the priest.

"It must be because I am so vain and wicked," answered Mariana between her sobs.

When he heard this the kind priest told her to come to Confession to him every week, and that he would see if she were really trying to be good and to prepare her soul for receiving Jesus in Holy Communion. He also told her to beg Our Lord to come into her heart, especially when she saw others going to receive Him. Jesus would come into her heart spiritually, he explained to her, if she really wished to receive Him.

Mariana did just as the priest had told her to, and after each Spiritual Communion Jesus filled her heart more and more with His divine love, so that the child often remained long hours in prayer, talking to her beloved Jesus. By the Feast of Our Lady's Assumption the wise priest gave Mariana permission to make her First Holy Communion.

Never was there such a happy little girl as she was when the morning of the Assumption dawned. In reward for all her desires Our Lord filled her heart to overflowing with His love and grace. Mariana used to say afterwards that no matter how long she lived she would never forget the happiness of her First Communion day. Until she was fifteen she always went to Holy Communion three times a week, which was very often for a little girl in those days. All during those years she never forgot how she had once grieved her dear Jesus by her vanity, and soon after her fifteenth birthday was past she gave herself entirely to Our Dear Lord by becoming a nun. Perhaps it was in memory of her happy First Communion day that she took the name of Sister Mary of the Angels.

GEMMA GALGANI

ou have all heard of the great St. Paul, and of how he spent his life after his conversion in preaching "Christ and Him Crucified." Ever since the days in which this ardent apostle lived there have been saints in the Church who have honoured Our Dear Lord in His sufferings and who have been glad to suffer for love of Him. Just forty years ago a holy little girl was born to whom it was given to suffer for the love of Jesus many pains like those Our Blessed Lord suffered in His Sacred Passion. This story will tell you about her First Holy Communion, but when you are older you must try to learn more about her.

In a small village in Northern Italy, near the ancient city of Lucca, there lived a pious chemist whose name was Henry Galgani. He had five boys and three girls, who all died when they were young except three, who were still living in 1914. Their mother belonged to a noble Italian family, and on 12th March, 1878 her eldest daughter was born. She was baptized the next day, receiving the name of Gemma, which in English means "Gem"; and the little girl does indeed shine today as a gem in the Church of God.

To look at, she was just the same as any other little girl, but her soul was beautiful in God's sight. When she was only two years old she was sent to a school like a kindergarten during the day, but used to return home each night.

Gemma's mother was, as people say, "a saint." She taught her little daughter all about Almighty God, Our Blessed Lady, the angels and the saints. Often she used to show her a crucifix and say: "Look, Gemma, how this dear Jesus died on the cross for us."

And Gemma would eagerly listen to all her mother told her about the sufferings of Our Dear Lord, even following her about the house to say: "Mamma, tell me a little more about Jesus."

Before she was seven years old Gemma made her First Confession. But soon after this her mother became very ill. This was a great grief to Gemma. She used to kneel by her mother's pillow while they prayed together, till her father sent her away to be taken care of by a kind aunt. The little girl went without a murmur, but she never saw her dear mother again, for she died soon after.

Not very long after this Gemma was sent to school again, this time to a convent. Gemma was delighted, and a long time afterwards, speaking of it, she said: "I began to go to the school of the Sisters; I was in paradise." She very soon made friends with her companions, who learnt to love her dearly; and before long Gemma was the life and soul of the place.

Almost at once she asked to be allowed to make her First Holy Communion. Although nine years of age Gemma was very small for her age, so she was told she must wait a little longer. With tears she begged her father, the priest, and the Sisters to change their minds.

"Give me Jesus," she would say, "and you will see how good I shall be. I shall be quite changed. I won't commit any more sins. Give Him to me for I cannot live without Him."

At last the priest gave way and told her father that Gemma was quite ready to receive Our Lord into her heart.

"If we do not want our Gemma to die of longing," he said, "we must allow her to go to Holy Communion."

When Gemma heard this she thanked Our Lord and His dear Mother, and then asked to be allowed to live in the convent while she prepared herself for such a great act. Her father did not like to lose his little girl even for a short time, but she begged so hard that at last he said she might "just for ten days."

"Oh, how happy I was," wrote Gemma afterwards. "As soon as I got inside the convent I ran to the chapel to thank Jesus; and with all the earnestness I could I implored of Him to prepare me well for my Holy Communion. Then I felt," she adds, "an earnest desire to know all about the life and sufferings of Jesus."

This thought of the Passion of Our Blessed Lord with Holy Communion is the one He Himself asked us never to forget when He said to His Apostles at the Last Supper: "Do this in memory of Me." Ever since that day the Church has taught us to see in the Holy Mass one and the same Sacrifice with that of Our Lord on the Cross, and to think of His Passion when we go to Holy Communion.

Gemma learned all the good Sisters taught her about the sufferings of Our Blessed Lord and the mystery of the Blessed Sacrament. The priest used to give instructions to the First Communicants, and every day he repeated: "Whoever feeds on Jesus lives with His Life."

Gemma said afterwards: "I almost died of longing to be able to say those words: Jesus lives in me." The day fixed for her First Holy Communion was Sunday, the Feast of the Sacred Heart, 19th June 1887. On the Saturday before this happy day Gemma wrote to her father, and this is what she said:

"DEAR PAPA,—Today is the eve of my First Communion, a day for me of the greatest happiness. I write these few lines only to tell you of my love, and to ask you to pray to Jesus in order that the first time He comes to dwell in me, He may find me ready to receive all the graces He has prepared for me. I beg your pardon for all my disobedience, and all the pain I have ever given you, and I beg of you this evening to forget it all. I ask you to bless me. Your most loving daughter,
"GEMMA."

The next morning Gemma almost ran to the chapel, and during Holy Mass her dear Jesus came for the first time into her loving little heart. She kept very quiet and recollected all day, spending her time with Our Blessed Lord in chapel, or in talking of Him to the Sisters. She took a little time also to write down all she wished to promise Our Lord in return for His Gift of Himself to her. Here is what she wrote:

1. I will confess my sins and receive Holy Communion each time as if it were to be the last.
2. I will often visit Jesus in the tabernacle, especially when I am sad.
3. I will prepare for every Feast of Our Lady by some mortification, and every evening I will ask my Heavenly Mother's blessing.
4. I will try to remember that God always sees me.
5. Every time the clock strikes I will say three times: "My Jesus mercy."

Gemma kept all these resolutions, for she was resolved to become a saint.

The Sister who taught her at school often used to remind her of this and say to her "Gemma, remember that you must become a truly precious gem."

When she won the first place in her class this Sister rewarded her by telling her more about Our Lord's Sufferings and Death upon the Cross, and the little girl grew more and more in the love of "Jesus Christ Crucified."

In 1894 Gemma gained the Gold Medal Prize for Religious Knowledge. Long before this she had become a daily communicant, but when she was thirteen she became very ill and had to leave school.

At home, when she got better, Gemma went on trying to please Our Lord in all she did. Her great desire was to suffer for love of Him.

"Yes, my Jesus," she used to say to Him, "I wish to suffer and to suffer much for Thee." Later on Jesus granted her desire, and even allowed her the privilege of bearing in her body the marks of His Five Most Precious Wounds, as He did long ago to St. Francis of Assisi. For all this Gemma found grace and strength in Holy Communion.

JEAN BAPTISTE VIANNEY

About a hundred and fifty years ago there was born into this world a little boy who afterwards became a holy priest, and is now famous as the Blessed Jean Baptiste Vianney, the Curé of Ars. Ars is a tiny village in the south of France, and *curé* is the French for "parish priest." The little boy was not born at Ars, but at another village called Dardilly. His father lived in a farmhouse right in the midst of the most beautiful country. On one side of the farm were shady woods and deep valleys, and stretching far away in front of it were pleasant green fields and orchards. Jean Baptiste's father and mother were not rich, but they were both very good Catholics, who loved Almighty God and Our Blessed Lady with their whole hearts, and who took great pleasure in being kind to the poor and those in trouble, for the sake of Our Dear Lord, Who said: "Whatsoever you do to the least of these My little ones for My sake, you do it unto Me."

Before Jean Baptiste was born his mother had said that if Almighty God should send her another little boy (for she had already had one son), she would bring him up in a special way for the service of God. Soon after this God sent her a little baby boy, our Jean Baptiste. The same day he was born the child was baptized, so that from the very first moment he might belong to God, our dear Heavenly Father.

Long before he could walk his mother taught him to join his tiny hands in prayer, and to lisp the sweet names of Jesus and Mary. Each morning this good mother used to awake her children herself to make sure that their first thoughts and actions should be offered to God. She taught them to make a big Sign of the Cross and say:

> "My God, I offer Thee today
> All that I think, or do, or say."

During his whole life, and he lived to be quite an old man, Jean Baptiste never once forgot to do this. By the time he was three years old there was nothing he loved better than to be saying his prayers. He would kneel down in any quiet corner he could find, and, taking out his rosary, contentedly say his "Hail Marys." One of his first troubles was over this rosary. His little sister took a fancy to it, and wanted Jean Baptiste to give it to her. Naturally he wished to keep it for himself, as he used it so often, yet he did not want to be selfish. In the end he asked his mother what he should do.

"Give it to your little sister," she answered, "for the love of God."

Jean Baptiste shed a few tears over parting with his treasure, but did as his mother had said. This act gave him a new idea: he learnt that he could show his love for Our Lord and His Blessed Mother not only by saying his prayers, but also by giving up to others things that he liked.

Often, while he was still a little boy, Jean Baptiste's mother used to take him with her to church. During Holy Mass he said his prayers so well and kept so still that her friends would notice it, and say: "You must make a priest of that little one," and his mother would smile and pray that it might be so. But, alas! when Jean Baptiste was seven years old there was a Revolution in France—that is, a number of wicked men got all the power into their hands and wanted to do away with all order and religion.

Soon the churches were closed and priests were hunted from place to place, and put to death whenever they were found. Only very seldom could Jean Baptiste hear Mass during that dreadful time, and then it was in secret, in a barn or hay-loft, with someone watching outside to see that no one came to take the poor priest prisoner. But though he could not go to Holy Mass as he used to, Jean Baptiste could still say his prayers. His mother had given him a little wooden statue of Our Blessed Lady, and the boy carried it with him wherever he went. When he was eight he was given the care of his father's sheep and cows. He had to take them into the far meadows to feed on the sweet grass there. His little companions would often go with him, and when they reached the fields Jean Baptiste would put his dear statue on a hillock, or in the hollow of a tree, and then he with his companions would kneel in front of it and say their prayers. After this Jean Baptiste used to tell his companions all about Our Blessed Lady and her Divine Son. When the others were tired they would run away and play, but he stayed on to say his Rosary, or moved his little statue to a quieter spot. Sometimes he used to spend whole hours in this way.

At last, when Jean Baptiste was eleven years old, some Sisters came to a village near by to teach the children their religion, and Jean Baptiste was sent to live with his grandfather that he might be prepared for the Sacraments. He made his First Confession and then began to prepare for his First Holy Communion. He could not spend long hours praying now, for he was getting to be a big boy, and he had to do a great deal of hard work on the farm; but whenever he had a few spare moments he always spent them in prayer. Jean Baptiste knew that Almighty God was just as pleased with work when it is done for His glory, so he tried to do more and more work to please Him. He used to take his statue of Our Blessed Lady with him into the fields which he had to dig up, place it at a little distance from him, and then see how quickly he could dig his way to it. Then taking it up once more place it farther on, and begin again.

Not only did Jean Baptiste offer up his work in preparation for his First Holy Communion, but he gave away to God's poor (and there were many in those days of revolution) his food, and even his clothes, glad to go hungry or cold himself to show his love for God.

Now came the last happy days before his First Holy Communion. A priest was hidden in one of the farm-houses, and each night the village boys would quietly slip in, and seated on the floor at the priest's feet, would listen while he taught them all about this wonderful Sacrament. Then, when at last they were all instructed and prepared, a barn was chosen in which the priest could say Mass. Jean Baptiste and his young companions helped to load the wagons of hay which were placed outside the window and door so that no enemy might see what was going on inside. Late that night an altar was got ready and everything arranged for Mass. Very, very early in the morning, when everything was yet quite dark, Jean Baptiste and his family, with just a few friends, got up quietly and went into the barn, which was lighted by one or two candles.

All through the Mass Jean Baptiste knelt without moving, never once taking his eyes off the altar and the priest until the great moment when he and his little companions received Our Dear Lord for the first time. Returning to his place, his heart overflowing with love, Jean Baptiste offered his whole life and work for the service of Our Dear Lord, and Jesus accepted his offering and chose him to be a priest and to do a great deal for His Church.

He taught them all about this wonderful Sacrament

Soon after this the churches in France were opened again—the Revolution was over. Each morning Mass was said, but now Jean Baptiste had to work from early morning, and often he could not go to Mass, for he was paid for his labour and the work had to be done. So what did he do? He saved up all his money and all his little treasures, and with them he paid anyone who would work for him during the time he went to Mass and Holy Communion. Years after, when he was an old and holy priest, he would say that the happiest days of his life were those he spent just before and after his First Holy Communion.

BLESSED JULIE

More than a hundred years ago, in a little village in Picardy in France, named Cuvily, lived a father and mother and three little children, Madeleine, Julie and their little brother Louis. There had been four more little children but God had taken them to live with Him in heaven, and from there they looked down upon and watched over their father and mother and the three left on earth. When Julie was born, Madeleine was seven years old, and thought herself a big girl. While Julie was quite tiny, her mother used to show her pictures of Jesus and Our Blessed Lady, and taught her little prayers to say. If she took her for a walk they would go to the end of the village where there was a large crucifix with a little bench in front of it. Kneeling there with little Julie, her mother would tell her all that dear Jesus suffered for love of us. Then Julie's tears would flow, and she would ask her mother what she could do in return.

Later on she began to go to the village school. There the little girls and boys learnt the catechism and all about Almighty God. You should have seen Julie during those lessons; she did not play and fidget and look about, but with her eyes fixed on the schoolmaster she seemed to drink in every word he was saying.

By the time she was seven she knew every word of the catechism, and all the meanings too. Not so the other little children. Often they found it very hard and uninteresting, and they could not answer the questions. Little Julie noticed this, and it made her sad. She loved Our Lord so much that she wanted all the others to know and love Him too. Often when they were playing in the fields little Julie would get the others all round her, and with her catechism on her knee she would explain it so well, and tell them such wonderful things about Almighty God, that they were all delighted and were always glad to listen. Sometimes Julie would notice that certain little boys and girls were not there, and she would send the others to look for them.

"I want plenty of little souls," she would say, "to teach them to love the Good God."

There was a very holy priest in that village,

and he soon noticed what a good little girl Julie was, and how much she loved the Good God and was loved by Him in return. So he tried to help her to become even more holy. He taught her how to talk to our Blessed Lord when at church and at home, and how to give up little things she liked to show her love for Him. He taught her, too, how to watch over her temper. Julie's little brother Louis was a great tease, and sometimes Julie found it very hard not to speak crossly. She knew that cross words displeased Our Lord, so she prayed very hard for patience, and if ever she spoke a cross word she would at once say she was sorry. Very soon, no matter how much Louis teased, she was always gentle and patient, trying to be like her dear Jesus during His Sacred Passion.

When the good priest saw how hard Julie tried to correct her faults, and how well she prayed, he said he would let her make her First Holy Communion. But, in case the other village children should be jealous at Julie's being allowed to make it so much sooner than they, the good priest said she must keep it a secret. How happy Julie was, and how she longed for the day to come! At last the happy morning dawned, and you shall know just what happened.

Very, very early in the morning, before anyone was awake, little Julie got up. She put on the simple peasant's dress that she always wore, and her little bonnet, and opening her door very quietly, so as not to awake her brother, and sister, she ran quickly to the village church. The good priest was waiting at the door for her, and together they went in. How empty the big church looked, but it did not feel empty to Julie. She only had thoughts for her God waiting for her there in the tabernacle.

First she said the prayers for Holy Communion that the priest had taught her. Then she began to pray in her own words until the priest went up to the altar. Very reverently Julie knelt on a low rush-bottomed chair and received her First Holy Communion; no white frock or veil had she, no little companions kneeling at her side, no fathers and mothers watching, no sweet music nor bright flowers; but instead the church was filled with beautiful angels adoring their God, and looking with wonder on little Julie's soul, now become the home of their God and hers. And how happy was her guardian angel at her side now that Julie had Jesus in her heart! Long Julie remained there, thanking dear Jesus for the gift of Himself

How happy was her Guardian Angel at her side

that morning; and after this she thanked the kind priest for all the trouble he had taken with her, then quietly returned home to her ordinary day's work.

From time to time for two whole years Julie received Holy Communion in this way all alone. After that the priest allowed her to go with the other children of the village, but she never told the others her secret, and how many times already Our Lord had come to visit her.

When she grew up Julie never missed an opportunity of hearing Mass and receiving Holy Communion, no matter how many difficulties there were in the way. All her life long she taught others to know and love Our Lord in the Blessed Sacrament, and Jesus filled her heart full of love and joy in Him, so that she always kept singing in her heart "Oh, how good is the Good God!"

FIRST COMMUNION DAYS

AUTHOR'S PREFACE

Encouraged by the good wishes and kindly criticism of many who have used "True Stories for First Communicants" and have found them helpful, the writer ventures to place, side by side with the first, a second volume of stories. Like the first, they are all true, so they should satisfy even the "least of these little ones." That they may help to draw some of them closer to Him Who longed for children to come to Him is the writer's earnest wish.

First Sunday of Advent, 1919.

PREFACE

The hope expressed in the preface of the little collection of "Stories for First Communicants" is here in this volume fully realised. It contains a new series of tales similar and equal to those we so cordially welcomed about twelve months ago. We had hardly dared to expect that the hope and call for more could be so speedily answered. The promptness of the reply puts all little children and their teachers under a new obligation to the good Sister who selects for us such nice things from her storehouse of precious memories of the sayings and doings of baby Communicants. With these sets of stories at hand one can face with some confidence the difficult task of preparing our little children of six and seven for the Sacraments. This is the use the author has made of them, and, finding their value, has generously given them to the world. We trust the store is not yet exhausted.

W. Roche, S.J.

Octave of the Immaculate Conception, 1919.

JOSEPH

A Sister of Charity was one day visiting the family of a poor child attending the school of which she had the charge. In her hand she carried a basket of provisions, for the family were poor and in want. Up one street and down another trudged the good Sister. At last she came to a row of small shops, between two of which was a narrow passage leading into a small square court. Around this court were sheds or rooms, and in each of these dwelt a different family. As Sister Louise came out from the particular room she had come to visit, a woman standing in the doorway of the next one spoke to her.

"Sister," she said, "will you take my Joseph into your school? He's gone five, and the inspector's been round."

As the Sister stopped at the open door she had a view of the entire room and family. It was poorer than any of you could imagine. Half the room was occupied by a large but broken-down bed, the rest by a table and two boxes used for seats. The walls were hidden by various garments hanging from nails. The one small window was broken and had a piece of paper stuck over the hole. This was Joseph's home, where he slept and played and had his meals. The family were at that moment having their tea, the father seated on a box, the three children upon the bed. Two cups without handles were provided for the father and mother, but the children shared a saucer between them.

"Come here, Joey, and let Sister see you," said the mother.

Joey slid carefully off the bed, placed the empty saucer on the table, and stood beside his mother looking up at Sister Louise. His legs were bare, his little shirt and trousers ragged, dirty, and torn. His face was surrounded by a thick crop of rough yellow hair, making him look like a copy of shock-headed Peter.

"He's a fine boy is Joey," said the mother, looking with pride on her eldest son, while she tried to rub up his face with a corner of her apron. "He's that clever, there's nothing he can't do."

"Has he been baptised?" asked Sister Louise.

"Oh yes, Father John baptised him along with Mrs. Moore's Tom."

"Very well," said Sister Louise, "you may send him next Monday, but see that he is washed and tidy."

So the following week Joseph began his school life. His face had been washed and his little shirt too, otherwise he looked much the same as when Sister Louise had first made his acquaintance.

Joseph thought school a wonderful place, something like heaven, he told his mother. It was warm, there was plenty of room to move about, pretty pictures hung on the wall, and, above all, there was music! Joseph loved music; and a lady actually played music while Joseph and the other children marched around the room. Dinner hour came all too quickly, and when afternoon school was over, he cried because he had to go home.

His teachers became very pleased with him. He tried so hard at all his lessons that he was soon the first in his class. "If only he were clean and tidy," the teacher would say to Sister Louise, "we could do almost anything with him!"

Each morning as soon as he came into school, Joseph was sent to wash his face and hands; but he could not wash his clothes, which every day became more ragged and dirty. Two or three times Sister had given him a coat or a jersey, but the next day he would come back without it, saying that his father had sold it, as he wanted money to pay for something to drink.

It was the month of November; the children had been told about the poor souls in purgatory, and taught to say some prayers for them. In the school hall too, there was a box on the altar into which the children sometimes dropped a penny, for they were saving up to have a Mass said for the Holy Souls.

Joseph had never had a penny to spend, but he had often watched the others drop one in, and wished that he could do so too.

About this time Joseph became the happy possessor of his first penny. It came about in this way. His hair had become by this time so rough and untidy that Sister Louise asked his mother to let her get it cut. Permission being readily given, Joseph, accompanied by a big girl, set off towards the barber's shop. It was a bitter cold day, a sharp east wind was blowing, and the people in the streets drew their furs closely around them. Joseph had no furs, he had not even a coat, but though he shivered with the cold, it never occurred to him to complain. The barber looked with pity at the boy's scanty clothing and at his pinched and hungry-looking little face and when the big girl gave him the usual threepence charge, he took one of the pennies and placed it in the boy's hand, saying, "Here, laddie, go and buy yourself a bun, or some sweeties!"

Joseph thanked him, and then with his penny safe in his hand he trotted happily back to school. The door was just about to be locked, but Joseph slipped in and ran in great haste towards the altar. There with a sigh of satisfaction he dropped his penny into the box. Turning round, he saw the Sister near him.

"The barber gave me the penny for sweeties," he said, "and I buyed a Holy Soul out of purgatory instead."

Two years went by. Joseph could read and write; he was, as his mother had said, a clever boy, but so ragged and dirty that he always looked the most uncared-for in the whole school. But that did not worry Joseph. He loved his school, enjoyed all his lessons, especially his Catechism which taught him to love Our Blessed Lord. About this time Joseph made his first confession, and then began to prepare for his First Holy Communion. The church was not far from the school, and every day Joseph would slip in on his way home, and

"The barber gave me a penny for sweeties, &
I buyed a Holy Soul out of purgatory instead".

sometimes remain for a long time praying before the Blessed Sacrament. To do this he had each day to resist the temptation to play cards with the other boys on a neighbouring doorstep. This was a favourite game at that time: the boys would play for sweets, or nuts, or even for money, and Joseph had often been the winner of these coveted prizes. But Sister did not like the game; she told them it was a dangerous one for little boys, and often led to sin later on, so Joseph had decided that in preparation for his First Holy Communion, he would give up playing, and pay a visit to Our Lord in the Blessed Sacrament instead.

Although Joseph's father and mother never went to Mass themselves they had not quite lost their Faith, and were quite willing that their children should go. Every Sunday Joseph would get up, help to dress his younger brother and sister, and take them to the children's Mass; there he would kneel so still, and join so reverently in the prayers and hymns, that Our Lord must have loved him very much.

When the day of his First Holy Communion arrived, Sister told him that although it was into his soul that Jesus was coming, still out of respect for Him, his God, he should make himself as clean and tidy as was in his power. This he did, and Sister lent him a large jersey and some shoes and socks which made him look quite respectable.

"Jesus will hardly know me," he said, looking at himself with great satisfaction.

After this, Joseph went to Holy Communion every day. He would take a crust of bread in his pocket for breakfast, and eat it on his way to school from the church.

One day the school doctor came to examine the children. When Joseph came in and the doctor noticed his thin, stunted little body, and his ragged garments, he turned to the Sister saying:

"What a wretched, miserable, little object."

Joseph heard, and his face flushed. When the doctor had gone, he said, "Sister, Our Lord didn't call me 'a wretched, miserable, little object,' when I went to Holy Communion this morning, did He?"

"No indeed," replied Sister. "When Jesus saw you coming into church this morning He said, 'Here is my little Joseph. How I love to come into his faithful little heart!'"

Joseph's face flushed with pleasure at these words. Looking up into Sister's face, he said, "I will always be His faithful little Joseph," and Sister felt sure that he would.

ANNE CATHERINE

On the 8th September, 1774, Our Blessed Lady's birthday, a little baby girl was born, who that same day was baptised and received the name of Anne Catherine. The house where she was born was poorer than any you have seen in this country. Built of wood and mud, it contained only one square room, which was divided by partitions. A few old chairs, a table, a spinning-wheel, and some piles of straw and hay, which served for beds, formed the only furniture. There was no chimney; the smoke from the fire filled the room, where the family and their animals lived together.

Anne Catherine's father had to work hard for his living. He was both good and pious; everything around him reminded him of Almighty God. When Anne Catherine was hardly a year old, he would seat her on his knee when he came home from work at night, and taking her tiny hand in his, would teach her how to make the Sign of the

Cross, and to say the *Our Father*. When she could walk, he used to take her out with him in the early morning, and then when the sun rose, made her kneel down with him, while he, taking off his cap, would thank God for the gift of His beautiful sun. He would tell her not to lie lazily in bed after the sun had risen, instead of making use of its light as God intended; and Anne Catherine was never known to remain in bed after she first awoke in the morning.

Sometimes when they were thus in the field together he would lay his hand on her head and say: "Stop a minute, my child, and look at God's beautiful earth, all is so fair and wonderful"; or he would point to the little church in the distance and say: "Let us kneel down a minute and worship our God, hidden in the little tabernacle, in the church. He can see us all the time, and give His blessing to our work." If the Mass bell rang he would make his little girl join in heart with those who were present, and sometimes teach her to say some of the Mass prayers aloud with him.

In this way he taught Anne Catherine to offer up all she was doing to Almighty God, and often to thank and praise Him for His goodness. All through her life everything in God's beautiful world—the sun, the flowers, the trees, and rivers—reminded her of Him, and helped her to love Him more.

Her mother was pious as her father; she it was who first taught Anne Catherine the Catechism and many of her prayers. When sending her to play with the other children she used to say:

"If you children are good and play nicely together, the Child Jesus and His Holy Angels will come and join in your games."

Anne Catherine would then run out to play, thinking as she went of some game which the Little Jesus would like. Sometimes with the clayey soil she and the other children would make little statues or shrines; Anne Catherine was very clever at this. Another favourite game was to gather wild flowers, and then with these in their hands, to form processions in honour of Our Lady or the Saints, asking their Guardian Angels to be their partners while they sang hymns or said the Rosary aloud.

There was not, however, much time for play. From her earliest years Anne Catherine had to work very hard; indeed it was wonderful how much those tiny hands managed to do, helping her mother in the house or her father in the fields.

But all the time Anne Catherine was thinking of Almighty God. She seemed to feel Him near her, giving her the strength to do these duties. God was so pleased with this that He filled her mind with pictures of Himself when He lived on earth, or of His saints who had lived long ago, or sometimes of the souls in purgatory. These last pictures made the little girl feel very sad, and she would pray that the Holy Souls might soon be freed from pain and go to heaven; also she would think out all sorts of penances to offer up for their release.

When Anne Catherine was about four years of age, someone gave her a picture of Our Lady with the Infant Jesus in her arms. This was a great treasure. She carefully hung it up in one corner of the room, placing a block of wood in front to serve as an altar. Here she would bring any little toy or present she had received and leave it there for the Child Jesus, and great was her joy if the present disappeared, for she then thought that the Child Jesus was pleased and had accepted it.

Anne Catherine was a very lovable little girl; even when quite tiny she could not bear to see others suffering. If she met a beggar she would tell him to wait, while she ran to ask her mother for some food or clothing, willingly going without herself that others might be helped.

In this holy way did Anne Catherine pass the first seven years of her life until the time came for her first Confession. For this she was prepared with the other village children of her own age. Anne Catherine felt sure that she was the naughtiest little girl among them, and spent a long time in examining her conscience, and in trying to make an act of perfect contrition, yet the biggest sins she could remember were that once she had quarrelled with another little girl, and once she had made fun of someone; she thought much penance and mortification would be needed before the punishment due to these would be cancelled. Her parents had given her a few pence to buy a little white cake for herself after her first Confession, as was the custom in that country, but Anne Catherine gave hers to a beggar as a little mortification to atone for her sins.

Four years went by, and now the great day of her First Communion approached, on which she was to receive the Body and Blood of her Lord for the first time. The burning love of her heart knew no bounds; she felt that she would never be able to do enough in preparation for so great an honour; yet she was anxious to do all she could, so that her soul might be found more worthy to become a dwelling-place for Jesus Christ. She used to beg her parents with tears in her eyes to tell her of any sin that she might not have noticed, in order that not the slightest fault might remain unconfessed.

When the day of her First Holy Communion arrived, Anne Catherine never once raised her eyes the whole way to church, so that nothing might distract her mind from Almighty God. Her one prayer was that He would always help her to do His Holy Will in all things. She offered her body to suffer and work for Him, her mind to think on Him alone, and her heart that it might always burn with a great love for Him, and that it might be always so pure that He would love to dwell within it. God answered her prayer, and Anne Catherine became more and more holy, doing great things for Almighty God, and receiving wonderful favours in return.

CYRIL

He was just four when he first came to school, a sturdy little fellow with a face like an angel, big blue eyes, a halo of yellow curls, and the sweetest smile. Dressed in a pale blue tunic, he looked a perfect picture that first morning. All the other children immediately fell in love with him, each seeking the honour of sitting near him or showing him his way about. In the playground, chocolates and sweets were showered upon him until Sister thought it wise to warn them that too many good things would make him ill. Cyril took all this attention as a matter of course; in fact, he seemed to expect it, not showing the least shyness at so much attention. In school he was very good, and interested in all the Sister said. He tried to do whatever work was set for the others, and yet the reason the mother had given for putting him to school while he was still so young was that at home he was never out of mischief.

Cyril's home was a good half-hour's walk from the school. He had been told that he must never, never go out of the playground until his mother or nurse came to fetch him. He had twice already run away from nurse, his mother said, so after school they watched him very carefully till mother came.

For some weeks everything went well. Cyril enjoyed school life, and seemed none the worse for all the petting he received from the others, nor was he in a hurry to return home. But one day mother was late, nearly all the other little ones had gone; only Cyril and three others remained in the playground with one of the mistresses. Once or twice Cyril had run to look if mother or nurse were coming, but not seeing them had once more joined in the game. Presently one little girl fell down, scraping her knee. Picking her up, the mistress wished to bathe it, so she told the others to play quietly till they were fetched, or till she returned. No sooner had she left the playground than Cyril ran once more to the door to look for his mother. The street was deserted; no one was in sight. Why should he not go to meet her, he thought, and immediately he set out.

Five minutes later his mother arrived, but by that time the other children had been called for, and the playground was empty. Inquiries were made, but no one knew anything about Cyril. On returning to the playground and finding it empty the mistress naturally thought the children had been called for, even taking the trouble to look down the street for any sign of them.

In a great state, Cyril's mother set out to look for him, up one street and down another, then back home to see if somehow he had arrived there. Cyril's father went out and made inquiries at the police station. Nurse started once more towards school. Then, just as they were wondering what to do next, in walked the little culprit quite unconcerned, fresh, rosy, and smiling.

Hiding her great joy, the mother greeted him with a scolding: "You naughty boy!" she exclaimed. "How could you run away from school like that? I must give you a good whipping to make you remember to do what you are told."

When the whipping was over and the boy's sobs had ceased, the mother tried to make him understand how naughty and disobedient he had been. "Have I not told you over and over again," she said, "that you may never go into the streets alone?"

"I didn't go alone," he replied. "My guardy angel walked a'side me all the time."

"Who?" said his mother, not understanding him.

"My guardy angel. Sister said he was always at my side."

"Yes, that is true," answered his mother, "but I told you to wait for me, or nurse, and it makes your guardian angel very sad when he sees you disobey."

So Cyril promised that he would never again go home until someone came to fetch him.

The next morning, when his mother told Sister all about it, Sister said: "His guardian angel certainly took care of him in a wonderful way. Fancy a little fellow of four finding his way all that distance, and crossing those busy streets too!"

About a year after this there was a school concert. Cyril was chosen to represent the Little Infant Jesus. Dressed in a white robe trimmed with gold, a golden halo fixed behind his curls, he made such a pretty picture that after the concert everybody wanted to talk to him. It was after this event that Cyril took such an interest in his Catechism lessons. He was always wanting to know more about Little Jesus when He was a boy. He felt somehow that as he had represented Him in the concert, he ought to be more like Him every day. He would sometimes say, "Sister, what would Little Jesus do if He were me now?" Another time he said to one of the little girls, "You can never be as much like Little Jesus as I can, because you are only a girl and I am a boy like Him." He did not understand that it is by making our souls beautiful we become more like Jesus.

The next year, when the First Confession class was formed, he begged so hard to be allowed to join, that Sister consented.

Although Cyril was only six years old, he soon learnt the prayers and was able to answer all the questions asked to see if the children really understood what they were going to do. When the day came, not only did Cyril make his First Confession with the others, but afterwards with them was placed in the First Communion Class.

Little Cyril was delighted. Little Jesus, Whom he loved so dearly, was coming into his heart; now indeed it would be easy to become like Him, for would not Jesus be able to tell him what to do? His eyes used to shine with delight when Sister was giving them instructions. How he longed for the day to come. But alas! mother did not approve of Cyril making his First Holy Communion at all. Confession was all very well, but Holy Communion, that was a very different matter. She herself had been twelve years old, she said; able to understand what she was doing. Such a beautiful day it had been, full of joy and consolation—why, she loved to think about it even now. If Cyril made it while he was so young he would forget all about his First Communion Day.

Sister told her how it was the wish of the Holy Father that children should receive Our Lord before they had soiled their souls with any big sin, and that by the strength received in Holy Communion these little ones would be kept from ever committing many sins that other children fell into so often. She reminded Cyril's mother too, how Our Lord had rebuked St Peter for trying to keep the little ones away from Him. "Just think how much others love your little Cyril, how much they like to have him with them, and to talk to him, yet Our Lord loves him with a much greater love than theirs, and longs to dwell within him. Why wait until that innocent little soul has been stained with sin before you allow Jesus to enter into it?"

"But Cyril doesn't understand what he is doing!" argued the mother.

"He understands quite well that it is Jesus he will receive under the appearance of bread, and that is all that is really required, though of course he knows a great deal more than that. Let me call him in," Sister added. "I will put a few questions to him before you. You will be surprised how much he really knows, and how eager he is to receive this great Sacrament."

So Cyril was called into the room. Standing beside Sister, he answered question after question, clearly and without hesitation. When Sister told him that mother thought him too young to make his First Holy Communion, he turned towards her, his eyes filled with tears.

"Oh mother," he said, "you won't keep me away from Little Jesus, will you? I will be so good. Sister, do ask mother to let me make it."

His mother was surprised at his eagerness, and went away promising to think it over again.

But Cyril now gave her no peace. Each day he would ask, "Mother dear, you will let me make my First Holy Communion, won't you?" or, "Do let Little Jesus come into my heart," until at last mother consented, and Cyril was made happy.

He tried so hard to be good, and was so obedient that even his mother noticed the change, and told Sister how pleased she was. She told her too, how when she had taken Cyril to a party, he had refused to take any lemonade when it was passed round, that when afterwards she had asked him why, he had told her he wanted to offer it to Little Jesus on his First Communion Day, it was so nice. "But I expect he will be as naughty as ever, once it is all over," she added.

But mother was mistaken. Cyril went to Holy Communion as often as mother would let him after the first great day, and though of course he had his little faults, he never lost the desire to be just like Little Jesus, and tried so hard to be good that he was loved by all, both at home and at school. Above all was he loved by Our Dear Lord, Whom he tried so faithfully to please and to imitate.

ROSE

In one of our large towns in Lancashire there once lived, not many years ago, a father and mother with five sturdy little boys. The father had to work hard all day in a factory, but he was a big strong man, glad to be able, by his labour, to earn money for his large family, who had to be fed and clothed and housed. The mother used to take in washing, so she was very busy too.

As I said before, there were five little boys, but there were no girls. Their father, who had always wished for a little girl, daily paid a short visit to the Church of the Sacred Heart, which he passed on his way home, to ask Our Blessed Lady to obtain for him, from her Divine Son, a little daughter.

After a time, Almighty God sent him the dearest little baby girl, whom they called Rose. The father and mother were delighted, and they did not forget to say a very fervent prayer of thanksgiving.

As soon as Rose could run about and talk, she was sent to school with her brothers, who were all very fond and proud of their little sister. The five boys were all big and strong for their age, but Rose, on the contrary, was rather small, and so fair that often people thought her delicate, though really she had never known a day's illness.

Rose was very happy at school, and was loved by both teachers and children. She got on well with all her lessons, but liked none so well as the first, which was all about Almighty God and how to love and please Him. By the time she was five and a half, she knew as much as the biggest children in the infant school, and a good deal more than most of them. Imagine her delight when one day Father X., the parish priest, coming into the infant school to settle with Sister which children might begin to prepare for their First Holy Communion, decided that Rose might be allowed to attend the instructions, although she was a year younger than most of the others. It was to be decided later whether she might really make her First Holy Communion. Rose herself had several times asked to be allowed to make it.

Her father and mother were very proud that their little girl should be chosen so early, and they encouraged her to be very attentive. But Rose did not need much encouragement to be good. She was the most earnest in the whole class, and was able to explain many things to her brother, two years older, who was to make his First Holy Communion the same day.

When the priest came to examine the class a week before the day chosen, which was February 2nd, no one answered his questions as well as Rose.

February 2nd that year came on a Saturday, so the day before was a First Friday, and on the Thursday all the children of the parish were accustomed to go to Confession in preparation for their First Friday Communion.

There were always so many children to go to Confession that day, that priests living near used to come to the Church of the Sacred Heart to hear them. There were not enough confessionals for all the priests, so some of them sat on the benches, and the little ones would come and kneel at their feet to make their confession. Knowing how busy every one would be, Father X. arranged for the little First Communicants to go to Confession on the Wednesday, three days before their First Holy Communion, when he would be able to give them plenty of time; for very little children do not like to be hurried.

So on Wednesday afternoon the forty-six little First Communicants all made their confession, and during their thanksgiving made up their minds to be very good for the next two days, so that they would not soil their pure white souls. Rose went with the others to Confession. All the next day she was so quiet her mother was afraid she was going to be ill, but the real reason was that Rose was not feeling quite happy. On Wednesday evening her big brother had been teasing her, and at last Rose, getting impatient, had called him a horrid boy and given him a little slap, which made him laugh more, but Rose, running away upstairs to her bedroom, suddenly looked at the picture of the Sacred Heart over her bed, and remembered what she had done. All the next day she was sad at the thought of having, as she thought, spoiled the lovely white soul into which Little Jesus was to come.

Thursday went by. Friday morning came, when all the little children of the school who were able went to Holy Communion. That morning Father X. came into the school to make the final arrangements for the next day. Just as he was going out of the infant school, Rose ran up to Sister.

"Please, Sister," she said, "may I speak to Father X.?"

"And what do you want with Father X.?" asked Sister kindly.

"I've done a sin," she answered, "and I do want to go to Confession again, before to-morrow."

"Well, run along, and tell him all about it," said Sister. "He's in the next room now."

When Rose came in to the priest she found him talking to the bigger girls. Running up to him, she slipped her hand into his. The priest looked down and smiled.

"What do you want?" he asked. "Are you not one of the little ones who are making their First Holy Communion to-morrow?"

"Yes, Father," she replied, "but please I want to go to Confession first."

"How is that? Were you not able to go last Wednesday?"

"Yes, Father, but I've done a sin since then, and I do want my soul to be quite white when Little Jesus comes in."

"Ah! I quite understand," said Father X. "Now you big girls get on with your work for a minute or two, while I have a little talk with Rose." And taking her to the back row of desks he let her sit on his knee, while she whispered her trouble into his ear. Then blessing her, and telling her not to worry any more, he sent her back to class perfectly happy.

The next day Rose made her First Holy Communion with her brother and all her other little companions. It was the custom in that parish for all the little First Communicants to make a novena of Communions, that is, for nine days after their First Communion they received Our Blessed Lord each day.

This meant for little Rose getting up at a quarter-past seven to be in time for the quarter to eight Mass. She did not mind that at all; her only fear was that, when the novena was over, she might not be allowed to continue.

"May I go to Holy Communion every day, Sister?" she asked. "Even when the novena is over."

"Certainly, dear, if mother will let you," Sister replied.

And mother was quite willing, so day after day and week after week Rose received Daily Communion. When Good Friday came she was quite distressed at the thought of having to miss a day, and asked Sister if she thought the priest would let her receive Holy Communion if she asked him, and Sister had to explain that no Hosts are consecrated on the Day on which Our Lord died, and that only the dying may receive Holy Communion on Good Friday. Only one priest in each parish receives Our Lord in a Host consecrated on Holy Thursday.

All the summer term and through the holidays Rose never missed her Holy Communion even for one day. When the following winter came, her mother thought she ought to have a long sleep now and again, but Rose begged so hard to be allowed to get up that her mother did not like to refuse her. One day her mother came to school and asked Sister if she would persuade Rose to have a long sleep once a week.

"Is she not keeping well?" said Sister.

"Oh, yes," her mother replied, "she never has a day's illness."

"Perhaps she complains of feeling tired?"

"Oh no, she goes to bed at half-past six and sleeps soundly all night, but she is often asleep in the morning and it seems too bad to get her up in the dark every day."

"I don't think I should worry about that,"

replied Sister. "Holy Communion will do her more good than an extra half-hour's sleep."

So Rose was allowed to continue her Daily Communion.

But one day Rose went out to a party, and it was nearly eleven when she went to bed. The next morning at a quarter-past seven she was sound asleep, and her mother did not like to wake her. She slept on until the hands of the clock pointed to half-past eight, and then she awoke. Jumping out of bed she asked the time, but when she found she was too late to go to Mass and Holy Communion, she cried so bitterly her mother did not know how to comfort her, until, remembering that there was another Mass at half-past nine, she allowed her to go to that.

At ten o'clock Rose walked into school.

"Why, Rose," said Sister, "what has happened? This is the very first time you have been late for school."

Then Rose told her all about the long sleep and being too late for the quarter to eight Mass.

"I knew you'd excuse me being late, Sister, just this once," she said. "Mother will wake me up next time. I came to tell you, but please may I go home and have my breakfast now?"

And it really was the only time. Month after month slipped by. Rose went up to the big girls' school. She worked hard at home, too, helping mother, but no matter how tired she might feel, nothing could make her miss her Daily Communion.

JACKIE

It was Holy Saturday, and in the large cathedral of X. the Bishop was blessing the font, and the priests and people present were standing near. Presently the swing door opened and in toddled three of the tiniest children ever seen alone in church. The eldest looked barely three years old, and the baby could only just walk with the help of the other two. Not the slightest notice did they take of the priests or people, but solemnly wended their way up the middle passage of the church until they almost reached the altar rails. Here they stopped, and all tried to genuflect, the two elder babies making a big Sign of the Cross before entering the bench, where they knelt for the space of a "Hail Mary." Getting up, they walked a little farther on, and kneeling again with another large Sign of the Cross, entered a second bench, where they knelt for a very short prayer. Once more they went up still farther, and yet again, the fourth journey bringing them to the front bench. Now they seemed satisfied. They genuflected for the last time, and, just as solemnly as they had entered, they toddled down the whole length of the nave, pushed open the swing door, and disappeared.

That same morning, a lady, who had been in the cathedral and had noticed them there, met them just as she left the church. The two younger ones were seated in a perambulator, and the eldest, standing beside it, was evidently waiting for somebody in the shop.

The lady could not resist speaking to them.

"Are you not the three little children I saw in church?" she said. "Do you often go there to say your prayers?"

Three solemn pairs of eyes looked up at her, and the eldest replied:

"I take the little ones to see dear Jesus, so that He won't be lonely; mother says Jesus loves little children," and she looked with pride at her little brother and sister.

"And how old are you?" asked the lady.

"Nearly four," she answered. "Jackie's two and a half, and Baby is one and a quarter. We live next door to Jesus."

"I am sure dear Jesus loves to see three such good little children," said the lady, and slipping a penny into each little hand, she went on her way, leaving the babies examining their coins.

Two or three weeks later the lady noticed the same three little ones coming out from Mass with their mother. As they came to the church door they recognised her, and the little girl, pulling her mother's dress, said:

"That's the lady that gave us the pennies, mamma."

The lady turned and smiled at the children, saying:

"Ah! here are the three little friends of dear Jesus," and she told the mother of their little visit, and what pleasure it had given her to see them so reverent in church.

"They love going to church, even Baby," replied the mother. "Who lives in there, Baby?" she asked the little one in her arms, pointing to the church door.

"Dear Jesus," answered Baby, raising her little hand to blow Him a kiss.

Four years went by. All three children now attended school, for even Baby was five years old. One Sunday morning only the two little girls were at Mass. Auntie and Jackie were very ill, and mother had to stop at home to look after them, they told the lady, who was now quite an old friend of the little trio. The next Sunday they were alone again.

"Auntie has gone to heaven," said Mary. "Father Edwards brought Jesus out of church to our house, and Jesus took auntie back to heaven with Him."

"And Jackie wants to go too," said Annie. "He keeps asking mamma to bring him the priest."

"But mamma says he is too young," said Mary.

That day the lady went to see Jackie. The little child was lying in his bed, his face flushed with fever.

Jackie was very pleased to see the lady, and one of the first things he asked her was to bring him a priest.

"Won't you ask Father Edwards to bring me Jesus?" he said. "I do want Jesus."

The lady promised she would ask the priest to come, and Jackie was satisfied.

That same evening Father Edwards went to the house. He had a long talk with Jackie, who told him how much he wished to go to Holy Communion.

Finding that Jackie quite understood Who would come to Him in this Holy Sacrament, the priest told his mother that there was no reason why Jackie should not make his First Holy Communion, although he was only six years old and in those days children had to wait until they were twelve or thirteen.

How happy he was! Jackie made his First Confession, and before the priest left the house he promised to bring Our Lord the next morning.

Carefully Jackie's mother prepared the little room. Everything in it was dusted and put tidy. A nice white cloth was placed on a small table; a crucifix in the centre with a candle on either side formed the altar. There were some flowers prettily arranged, a glass of Holy Water, another little glass of water in which the priest could dip his fingers, and a small towel to dry them.

Jackie watched these preparations with great pleasure. He was too ill to speak much, but once or twice he said to his mother:

"It will be nice to go to heaven with dear Jesus, won't it, mother?"

"Yes, dear," she would reply, smiling at him through her tears.

Though Jackie was awake and in much pain a great part of the night, he never once complained, while the mother sat patiently by his bedside, doing all she could to give some relief to her dear little boy.

"Don't cry, mother," he said once, "Jesus will soon come now."

Early the next morning Mary, who had been watching at the window, ran in to say that the priest was coming.

Giving each of her little girls a lighted candle to carry, mother went with them to the front door, where they knelt down as the priest, bearing Jesus, came in.

They then led the way to the room where Jackie lay waiting in his little bed. He was too weak to move, but his eyes shone with joy. Jesus had really come. Jesus would take him to heaven, where there would be no more pain and suffering.

Mother and the two little girls and the lady, who had also come to see Jackie make his First Holy Communion, knelt near the bed. Very reverently Jackie received his dear Jesus. After a while the priest said aloud a few easy prayers that Jackie could follow, and then they all went downstairs, leaving him alone with his God, his eyes closed and his tiny hands clasped on his breast.

A short time after, his mother came up, a cup in her hand with something in it for Jackie to

Mother two little girls and the lady knelt, &
very reverently Jackie received dear Jesus.

drink. He lay just as they had left him, only his eyes were open and a sweet smile was on his lips; but, as his mother came nearer, she saw that only her child's little body lay on the bed. Jesus had indeed taken Jackie to live with Him in heaven.

PETER

There were three of them, Peter, John, and Joseph; fair-haired, rosy-cheeked brothers, never still for a minute, their blue eyes sparkling with fun and mischief. Peter, the eldest, was six, and thought himself a very big boy in comparison with his two little brothers, one of whom was only three, and the other four years of age. Two hours each morning the little boys spent with their nursery governess, after which they were taken for a daily visit to grandmother, who lived at the other end of the town, and who kept in her cupboard a large box of preserved fruits thickly coated over with sugar. At some time during the morning visit this box was taken out, and each of the little boys invited to choose one of these tempting fruits. No wonder they looked forward to their daily walk.

In the afternoon the three boys played together in the garden, while nurse sat near mending socks. One afternoon, finding she was in need of

128

more wool, nurse left her charges playing on the lawn while she went into the house to fetch some. She had only meant to be gone one moment, but she found so many things waiting to be put straight in the nursery, that half an hour flew by unheeded.

The three little boys had watched nurse disappear into the house, and instinctively when left alone, they looked round for some piece of mischief. Peter caught sight of the apple trees at the end of the garden. They had been forbidden to touch the apples many a time, but Peter had forgotten this.

"Come along, John," he cried, "let's get some apples."

The two younger boys scrambled to their feet and hastened after Peter. Alas! the tempting green fruit, which nurse would say was not ripe yet, hung just beyond their reach. Peter tried lifting up Joseph, but still they could not reach. Then he espied a long stick leaning up against the arbour.

"Now we'll have them," he shouted, and with a few blows soon succeeded in knocking off half a dozen.

Taking an apple in each hand, the three children returned to their seat on the lawn, and for a short time nothing was heard but the munching of sour apples.

When nurse returned she praised them for being so good and quiet while she was upstairs, and said she was glad she could trust them. But that evening little Joseph became so ill, that they had to send for the doctor. Mother made anxious inquiries about what he had been given to eat. Both nurse and cook declared that the children had eaten nothing but the plainest food; they had not even had any sweets that day, added nurse.

"I wonder if he could have found any poisonous berries in the garden," said mother.

At the sound of the words "poisonous berries," Peter, who was listening, trembled with fear. Were unripe apples poison? Supposing Joseph should die, it would be his fault.

"Oh, mamma," he cried, "I didn't know they were poison. We all eat them, two each. Shall we die?"

"What did you eat?" said mother, looking very anxious.

"Poisonous berries off the apple tree," sobbed Peter. "I knocked them off with a stick when nurse went indoors, and we had two each."

Mother could not help smiling at the idea of the poisonous berries on the apple tree, though the sour green apples had certainly managed to make little Joseph very ill indeed.

Sitting down on a chair, she took Peter on her knee, and tried to show him how wrong it was to disobey, and how it was still worse to teach his little brothers to be naughty too. How often had they been told not to touch the apples, and yet no sooner had nurse turned her back than they disobeyed. Mother tried to show him how, when nurse or mother were not there to look after them, Peter should take their place, and be like a little guardian angel to them.

Peter listened gravely to all she had to say, then throwing his arms around her neck he said:

"I will be good, mother. I'll never teach them to be naughty again," and a little later, when saying his night prayers, he added: "Dear Jesus, help me to be a guardian angel to John and Joseph, and please don't let Joseph die this time."

Whenever it was possible mother used to put her three little boys to bed herself. First they used to have a little talk together, when mother would tell them about Our Dear Lord and Our Blessed Lady; then they would tell her what they had been doing during the day, and whether they had been good; then when they were just ready for bed, they would all three kneel down together and repeat after her their baby night prayers.

Christmas came, and soon after Peter made his First Confession. For some time mother had been teaching him his prayers, and explaining to him all about this wonderful Sacrament.

"I've done such a lot of sins I 'spect I shall get a very big penance," he said.

But his mother told him how Our Lord had suffered and done penance for our sins, but that we should try and do a little ourselves to unite with His. She told him too, that the priest only gave a very small penance in Confession, leaving the rest to our love.

About this time Peter began to object to saying his prayers with his little brothers. "I can't think when they are saying the words after me," he would say. "May I go into your room to say them, mother?"

So when the time came for prayers, the two little ones still knelt at mother's knee, but Peter knelt in front of the little altar in mother's room, where he could talk to God properly, he said.

Just before Lent, mother had been telling the three little boys about Our Dear Lord's sufferings. She had also tried to explain to Peter how during Lent it was the custom to give up something nice in order to be more like Him, Who gave up everything for love of us, and also in order to do penance for sin.

"What could I give up, mother?" he asked.

But mother told him he must choose for himself.

Peter thought and thought. At last he decided that a very good penance would be to give up the preserved fruit out of grandma's box each day. The next evening he told his mother he had chosen his penance, and told her what it was. Mother kissed him and hoped he would not find it too hard.

"It will make up for taking the apples and making Joseph ill last year," he replied.

The next week Lent began. On Ash Wednesday Peter went to church with mother, but the next day the boys went for their usual visit to grandma's.

That very morning a new box of preserved fruit was opened for the children. How delicious they looked! John and Joseph soon chose theirs, but to grandma's surprise Peter walked quickly away to the window, saying.

"No thank you, grandma, not to-day," and he pretended to be very busy watching a robin in the garden.

Keeping his eyes away from the tempting
box, Peter resisted his desire for the fruit.

"Why, are you not feeling well, my dear boy?" asked grandma, quite concerned.

"Oh yes, thank you, grandma," he replied, carefully keeping his eyes away from the tempting box.

The next day came, and again Peter resisted the desire for his share of the fruit, but that evening he told his mother that he never thought it would be so hard to give it up.

"You are quite free to take the fruit as usual if you wish," said his mother. "Do you not think it would be better to choose something easier?"

But Peter would not hear of changing.

"No, mother," he replied, "I want to do something hard. It will show Jesus that I really do love Him. He did much more for me."

The next day mother told grandma all about it, so after that, although each of the little ones had their usual fruit, she never pressed Peter to take one. As soon as he caught sight of the box he would walk over to the window till it had disappeared again inside the cupboard, and each day he found it cost him less to give it up, till at the end of a fortnight he told his mother he didn't mind nearly so much now.

Both mother and grandma were very pleased with Peter, and they felt sure that Our Lord loved him very dearly for his self-sacrifice.

When Easter Sunday came, his grandma, besides his usual present, gave him as much money to put in the box for the orphans as the fruit would have cost. "So that you can actually give it to Our Lord," she said.

Peter was delighted, and though he had many nice presents that day, he said that he liked that one best of all.

Peter was now getting ready for his First Holy Communion. It was to take place on the Feast of Corpus Christi, and curiously enough that year it fell on Peter's seventh birthday.

Very carefully did he prepare for this great day. It was his first thought in the morning and his last at night. Each morning when coming home from their walk he would ask nurse to go by the road that passed the church so that he might just go in and pay a short visit to Our Lord in the Blessed Sacrament.

When mother asked him about having his little friends to tea for his birthday, he said, "Please, mother, may they come the next day? I just want only Jesus for my birthday," and his mother was very pleased with his suggestion.

Corpus Christi came, and mother and father and Peter all knelt at the Communion rail together, Peter receiving his dear Jesus for the first time. He spent the day very quietly, not even the arrival of numerous presents seemed to take his thoughts away from the happiness of the morning, and a few days later when the First Communion and the birthday party were both past events, Peter would say that on no day had he ever felt so happy as on Corpus Christi.

BETTY

Betty was a dainty little maid, her fair hair curled prettily over her shoulders, her blue eyes sparkled with fun, and though her clothes were poor and often patched, still they were always clean and tidy, for Betty was very particular about her appearance; she would not go to school in a torn or dirty frock, and many a night her mother (whose own clothes were anything but nice) would stay up late, washing, ironing, or mending for Betty, as she had no money to buy her new ones.

Betty's father, it is true, often earned good wages and would leave his work with plenty of money in his pocket, but alas, very little of it arrived home; for before he got there, he would have met some of his friends, and together they would go into a public house, and there sit for hours talking and drinking, until all, or almost all, the money was spent.

Betty's mother worked hard too, but most of the money she earned had to pay the rent or buy food, so there was little enough left for new clothes.

Betty was a Catholic, so were her father and mother, though no one would have thought it, for not one of the three ever went to Mass, nor entered a church to say a prayer. Her father spent Sunday morning in bed. Betty and her mother both got up very late, and then spent the rest of the morning in putting things straight, and preparing the dinner.

Betty took all this as a matter of course. Over and over again the Sister in school had told the children about going to Mass on Sundays, but somehow Betty had thought it never mattered about her, until one day in June.

That day, the Sister had been telling them of the love of the Sacred Heart, how great is His love for us, and how little He is loved in return. She told them, too, how the dear Sacred Heart was beating with pleasure at the thought of the visit of His little friends at the Holy Mass, how often so many disappointed Him, Sunday after Sunday, and yet He still waited on. Would they still go on being such a disappointment to Him? Was there one little child present here to-day who would sadden the dear Sacred Heart again next Sunday?

Betty felt her cheeks growing red and hot; her eyes filled with tears, two or three dropping unnoticed on the desk; she seemed to see Our Lord's Sacred Eyes looking right into her own. Ah! she had never thought of His love for her before; every Sunday He had been waiting, waiting, and each time she had disappointed Him. Never, never, would she miss Mass again.

The following Saturday night Betty told her parents that she was going to Mass the next morning and every Sunday in future.

"I shall never miss Mass again," she said.

"But I can't spare you, child," said her mother. "There's so much work to be done on Sunday mornings."

"Don't think yourself better than your parents," said her father. "We don't want any of that nonsense here."

Betty did not answer, but in the morning she got up very quietly so as not to disturb her father and mother, and set off to church for an early Mass.

She came home, her face beaming with happiness. She had not disappointed Jesus this time.

Betty began to tidy up the room, for her mother was not yet down. When an hour later she appeared, the first thing she noticed was the child's happy face, but somehow this only made her cross.

"Be quick and wash those plates," she said, "and let's have no more of your nonsense. Your father was fine and angry when he heard you go out this morning. I wouldn't be you when he comes down."

But when father did come down, he seemed to have forgotten all about it, for not a word was said, and the week passed by as usual.

The next Saturday, however, showed that, though he had said nothing, he had not forgotten. Soon after Betty had gone to bed, he came in, and the first thing he asked his wife was whether Betty had said anything about going to Mass.

"Yes," she replied, "she told me she was going, though I promised her a beating if she did."

"No," he said, "you'll not beat her. I know a better way than that. I'll hide her boots. She thinks so much of her looks and her clothes, she's a deal too proud to go to church in bare feet."

That night when he went upstairs, he took Betty's boots from the side of her bed, and locked them up in the cupboard, putting the key in his pocket.

The next morning Betty got up very early. Father and mother were both asleep. Dressing herself quietly, she at last missed her boots, and began looking everywhere for them. At this moment her mother opened her eyes and saw her standing there.

"You can get back into bed, Betty," she said. "Your father has locked up your boots, so you can't go."

But Betty did not get back to bed. She went downstairs and began hunting for something to wear; but in vain. One pair each was all that any of them possessed. What should she do? Surely Our Lord would not want her to go to Mass without her boots! But this thought reminded her of the many, many times she had disappointed Him. What a splendid way this would be to make up!

Without another moment's hesitation, she took up her hat and ran out of the house in her bare feet. Up one street and down another she ran, and then suddenly stopped at the sight of two little school companions who stood at the corner of the street looking at her.

Betty felt herself growing redder and redder. What should she do? They would be sure to tell the others in school, and what would they think? Many of the children there were very poor, but there was not one who had not a pair of boots, or who went to school in bare feet.

It was too late to go back now. The two children had already gone on towards the church, and Betty followed them. Once or twice she saw them looking back at her.

As soon as Mass was over, she slipped out as quickly as possible and ran all the way home without once stopping.

Her mother was too astonished even to scold her, and her father could hardly believe she had really been to church at all.

"She may have done it once," he said, "but she'd not have the courage to do it again. You say she looked quite scared when she came in?"

The next day Betty's worst fears were realised. Quite a number of little girls were grouped together in the playground as she entered, and in the middle of them stood the two whom she had met the day before.

When Betty entered, several turned and looked at her feet, and she heard one say:

"It couldn't have been Betty, she's wearing her boots now."

"But it was," replied the other, and she called out, "Betty, didn't you go to Mass in bare feet yesterday?"

At that moment Sister came into the playground, and Betty, who thought she had heard the question, ran up to her crying: "I couldn't help it, I couldn't help it."

It was quite a little time before Sister could make out what was the matter, but when at last the tale was finished, she told Betty how proud she was of her, and that she was sure Our Dear Lord was very pleased with her too; she also promised the little girl that if she continued going to Sunday Mass she should very soon make her First Holy Communion, for Sister did not think the boots would be locked up again, as that had not prevented the brave child from going to Mass.

So Betty was comforted, and more determined than ever not to disappoint Our Lord.

But Sister was mistaken in thinking the boots would not be taken away again. Sunday after Sunday Betty's father locked them up, thinking each week she would at last give up going, for he knew Betty well enough to know what it must cost her to go out in her bare feet.

But Betty was brave, and though each Sunday she felt that everyone was looking at her feet, yet she would not be conquered.

At last it came to the very week when she was to make her First Holy Communion. There were only three little girls to make it with her, for the others had made theirs a few weeks before. The day arranged for was a Sunday. Betty would have no boots! What was she to do? She would appeal to her father's love, for she knew that in spite of everything he loved her dearly.

That night when he came home from work, Betty went up to him, and putting her arms around his neck, kissed him two or three times. Her father put his arm around her and drew her on to his knee.

"Father," said Betty, "next Sunday I am going to make my First Holy Communion. Please don't lock up my boots. You wouldn't like me to make my First Holy Communion in bare feet, would you?"

Her father did not at first reply. He had really been feeling very ashamed of himself for the last few weeks, when he saw how very bravely his little daughter had overcome her pride in order to do her duty.

"Why do you want to go to Mass?" he said at last, and then Betty told him of Our Lord waiting there Sunday after Sunday, and how she could not go on grieving Him as she had once done. "Oh, father," she said," if only you would come too!"

Her father's heart was touched.

"Little one," he said, with tears in his eyes, "you have conquered. Next Saturday come to meet me

Betty put her arms around his neck, "How happy you have made me Father," she said.

at my works and together we will go to the church, and I promise to be a better father to you."

Betty put her arms once more around his neck.

"How happy you have made me, father," she said.

Her father kept his promise. On Saturday, as he came out from his work, there was Betty waiting for him, and together they went to church and to Confession, and what is more, that very evening mother was persuaded to go too.

How happy was Betty the next morning! Sister had lent her a white frock and a veil, and father had polished up her boots till they shone. There was no need to worry to-day about her clothes, and indeed she had no time. She had so much to tell the Sacred Heart, Who had been lovingly watching and helping her through these trying weeks. And how well rewarded she felt for her little self-sacrifice, when she saw her father and mother go up to the altar rails and receive their God Whom they promised to serve more faithfully in the future.

CLEMENT CATHARY

Clement was a little French boy, who was born about a hundred years ago in the village of Moux, near Montpellier. His father, who was a blacksmith, was an honest, hard-working man, but unfortunately he no longer went to church, and had even given up saying his prayers. His mother went to Mass on Sundays, and to Holy Communion at Easter, but that was all. In fact at that time there were very few people in the whole village who really loved Our Blessed Lord, which made it the more remarkable that Clement should grow up good and pious, as he did.

Clement was born on a Tuesday, 23rd December, 1828, the day of the week that is dedicated to the Holy Angels, and certainly his Guardian Angel watched over him in a very special manner, protecting him when in danger, and guiding him through many a difficulty. Clement was a strong and healthy baby, and as he grew older he was very quick and clever both at lessons and at games.

Always the top of his class and carrying off the prizes, he was yet so gentle and amiable that he was loved by all, both old and young.

Though later he became a very holy man, and devoted his whole life to Almighty God, Clement did not become good all at once, and he had many a hard fight against temptation, doing wrong just like little boys do nowadays, and little girls, too. He, himself, tells us of two very naughty things he did when he was little, and they help to show us how hard he must have tried in order to become as good as he did, though after he had made his First Holy Communion, we never hear of him being naughty on purpose.

The first fault was committed when he was three or four years of age. One day he happened to pass a cart on which was placed, for sale, a large quantity of dates. Clement, after looking round and seeing that no one was near, filled his little blouse with the fruit, and then walked away eating the dates as fast as he could, when suddenly he met his father.

"Where did you get all those dates?" asked his father.

Knowing that he had done wrong, and afraid of being punished, Clement replied by telling a lie.

"Madame Tessine gave them to me," he said.

Madame Tessine was the owner of a little shop where Clement's mother bought her vegetables, and she had from time to time given Clement an apple or a nut, but his father knew that she would not have given him so many dates, and taking him by the hand he said, "I see I have a thief for my son. Come with me and we will go to Madame Tessine."

The shame he felt when his father reproached and corrected him before Madame, made Clement realise so well how wrong it was to steal and then excuse himself by telling a lie, that never again was he known to touch anything that did not belong to him; and so sorry was he for this fault, that when he was older he never passed a day without giving up something at his meals to make up, as he said, for his greediness when he was a little child.

The second fault, which he tells us about, happened about two years later, and might have ended very sadly if God had not protected his baby brother in a remarkable way.

When Clement was six and a half, God sent his mother another little son, who was called Adrian. One day, leaving her baby boy asleep in his cradle at the top of the house, his mother went downstairs to prepare the dinner. Presently the child awoke and began to cry.

"Run upstairs, Clement, and rock the cradle," said his mother.

"No," replied Clement, "I'm not a girl. Boys and men don't rock cradles."

His mother, unable to leave what she was doing just then, tried to coax him to go, but still he refused. Then she threatened to punish him, if he did not obey.

"Very well, I will go," said the naughty boy, "but I will rock so hard that the baby and cradle will tumble down," and up he went.

The cradle was an old-fashioned one, mounted on high rockers, and a fall from that would probably cost the baby its life.

After a little rocking Baby stopped crying, and soon fell asleep, but Clement, who was still in a very bad temper, then gave the cradle such a violent push that the baby was thrown out and the cradle overturned.

The poor mother, hearing the noise, rushed upstairs quite expecting to find her baby killed, for she had guessed by the sound what had happened. To her great joy she found the little boy quite uninjured, and so engrossed was she in soothing its cries, that Clement was forgotten until the father's return, when he received the punishment he had so well merited.

About this time Clement began to attend the Catechism class with the other village children, but he was so clever that in a very short time he not only knew all the answers, but could give the explanations, better than any of the bigger boys present.

Clement now began to feel a great desire to be a better boy. He took more trouble to say his prayers well, and to be obedient to his parents. At this time, too, he felt a great love and attraction to Our Blessed Lady growing in his heart. "I want to be her own little boy. I want to belong to her in a special manner," he would say to himself, and he would kneel at her altar, and looking up into the face of her statue there, would wonder what he could do to please her.

About the time of his eighth birthday he went to the parish priest.

"Father," he said, "I want to belong to Our Lady, to belong to her in a special way. What can I do?"

"I am pleased to hear you say that," replied the priest, "for if you will only give yourself to

Our Blessed Lady and try to please her, she will protect you through your whole life. Take this prayer, it is the one used by St Aloysius Gonzaga, go and kneel at Our Lady's altar and read it slowly, trying to mean every word you say."

Clement took the prayer and did as the priest had told him.

"As I knelt there" he said, "my soul was filled with joy. I felt that Our Dear Lady had indeed accepted me, and from that day my life was changed. I wished only to live for her and her Divine Son."

Three years after, the time fixed for his First Holy Communion drew near. Each day Clement knelt at Our Lady's altar and begged her to help him to prepare well for that great event. Day by day the First Communicants went to the good priest's house for instructions. Clement had the special charge of his cousin, a boy of his own age who had the misfortune to be blind. Each day Clement would go to his house to fetch him, and he looked after him so carefully and so kindly that everyone was touched. During the three days' retreat that the children made, and even on the First Communion day itself, Clement did everything for his blind cousin, but this did not prevent him from praying so fervently himself, that many of the villagers noticed him.

"Ah yes," said one man, "they pray well now, but once their First Communion is over they forget all about it, and are no better than they were before."

Clement heard this remark, and it made a great impression on him.

"They shall see," he said to himself, "whether I am no better than before," and taking a piece of chalk he wrote on the walls and on the door of his room: "Clement belongs to God for ever."

Never again was he the same reckless, heedless boy he had been, though he still remained eager at his studies and eager at his games. He was always happy, joyous, and light-hearted, offering up all he did, whether work or pleasure, for the greater glory of God. Later on he worked for God as a holy priest and a Jesuit, at first in his own country, and afterwards at the foreign missions.

JANE

ane and Mary were great friends, but though they lived next door to each other, they did not go to the same school. Jane went to a school just at the end of the street. Mary, who was a Catholic, had two roads to cross to get to hers, so that her mother always took her there, and fetched her home again, while Janie could go by herself.

After school Janie would wait to see if Mary and her mother were passing, and then if she saw them, she would run to meet them to ask if Mary could play with her after tea, and many a happy hour they spent together.

One Saturday, Mary in her turn asked her mother if she might invite Janie to tea, and great was her delight when the permission was given. Early that afternoon Jane arrived, and Mary showed her all her treasures. There was her best doll, generally kept in mother's drawer, as well as two others, one of which she lent to Janie for the afternoon. Picture books, too, were brought out and a pretty blue Rosary, which Janie thought was a necklace. After this, they each took a doll in their arms and went into the little garden to play, until Mary's mother called them in to tea.

To Jane's surprise, before they sat down, Mary and her mother made the shape of a cross on themselves, and Mary said some words aloud. Jane did not like to make any remark about it before Mary's mother, but after tea she asked Mary what she had said.

"I was asking God to bless my food," said Mary. "Catholics always do that."

"But why did you draw a kind of cross on yourself?" said Jane.

"It *was* a cross," Mary answered. "Our Lord died on a cross, and that's His sign. Look, I'll teach you how to make it."

Then and there Mary taught her friend to make the Sign of the Cross.

Janie was delighted, and very soon learnt both how to make the sign and to say the words.

"You should never be ashamed to make the Sign of the Cross," said Mary. "It's God's sign."

"I never will," replied Janie.

The next morning, as Janie and her father and mother were about to sit down to breakfast, Jane remembered what she had learnt the evening before, and standing up made a big Sign of the Cross, saying the words aloud.

"What are you doing, Janie?" said her mother.

"I'm asking God to bless my food, mother. Mary and her mother always ask God to bless their food, and they make a cross on themselves because Christ died on the cross for them, and it is His sign."

Janie's father and mother looked at one another. They had no wish for their little girl to copy her Catholic friend, but as they had never taught her any grace themselves, they did not like to forbid her to ask a blessing on her food, so they said nothing more about it.

After that day Mary often told Janie about the instructions she had in school, and even taught her the prayers and a short hymn, until after a while there was very little that Mary knew which Janie did not know too. The two friends liked these talks better than any of their other games. They called them "playing school." Mary was the teacher, and Jane was the child; they were both very much in earnest.

Standing up Janie made a big sign of the
Cross "I'm asking God to bless my food".

Janie never forgot now to say her prayers either morning or evening, and sometimes when her mother was putting her to bed, she would tell her some of the wonderful things she had heard about Jesus and His Blessed Mother.

"Why don't you and Mary play proper games?" Janie's mother would say. "You two are far too young to be talking about religion. You should be playing with your dolls."

"We do sometimes, mother," said Jane, "but they're only pretence, and religion is real. Don't you like to hear about God, mother?"

"Yes, on Sundays, sometimes. Only I'm generally too busy to go to church. I've your father's dinner to get ready."

"Mary always goes to church on Sundays. If you're too busy to take me, mother, may I go with her?"

"I should think Mary sees enough of you all the week. You always seem to be with her nowadays."

But Mary was quite willing that Jane should come with her, and so the very next Sunday, instead of telling her to sit quiet and look at her picture books, Janie's mother dressed her in her best clothes, gave her a kiss, and told her she might go "just this once."

"Be sure to behave nicely," she said, "or Mary will be sorry she has taken you."

Janie was very quiet during Holy Mass, but she used her eyes and ears well. She knew that she must not talk in church, but she meant to ask Mary about everything she had seen and heard when they came out; and Mary was quite ready to answer all her questions.

She told Janie about Jesus living in the Tabernacle, and how He was offered up to God during Holy Mass, just as He offered up Himself on the cross. She also told Janie how He came into people's hearts in Holy Communion.

"He came into my heart this morning," she said, "for I went to Holy Communion this morning with mamma and daddy before breakfast."

"May I go to Holy Communion?" said Janie eagerly.

"Oh no! you can come to Mass with me, but you can't go to Holy Communion, because you are not a Catholic."

"I wish I could be one," said Janie, "but mother doesn't want me to."

When Janie returned home dinner was ready, and during it father and mother had to hear all about Mass, and Holy Communion, and everything else that Janie had seen and heard. Then after dinner, when everything was cleared away, and father and mother were resting in their easy-chairs, she sang them the little hymn that Mary had taught her the week before. She had a pretty little voice, and sang it so nicely that her father was delighted.

"Don't you and Mary ever do anything but pray and sing hymns?" he asked.

"Oh yes, father, we skip and run races, and then, when we are tired, I ask Mary to play school, and tell me more about Jesus."

"It doesn't seem natural to me," said her mother. "I never thought about things like that when I was a little girl."

"Oh, don't worry, mother," said her father, "they'll soon grow tired of it and think of some other amusement."

About six weeks after this Janie came home from school feeling very ill. Her head was burning and her throat was sore. Her mother put her to bed and went for the doctor, for many people in their street had the influenza and she was afraid that Janie might be getting it too.

The doctor came, and when he had seen Janie and felt her pulse, and looked at her tongue, he told her mother that she certainly had a touch of influenza, but that he hoped it would be a mild attack and that she would soon be well again.

Janie was very good and patient. She took the medicine that the doctor sent without a murmur, though it was very bitter, and she did everything her mother told her.

For four days she was very feverish. On the fifth day the fever left her, but it seemed to take with it all Janie's strength, leaving in place of a plump, rosy-cheeked girl, a pale-faced little invalid, too weak even to sit up in bed, unless mother's arm was round her.

She had a little prayer book with Holy pictures in it, which Mary had given her, and she liked her mother to read to her out of it.

"I wish Mary's priest would come and make me a Catholic, mother," she would say, over and over again.

At last her mother went to Mary's house and told her friends how Janie kept wishing to see a Catholic priest, and asked if they thought one would come to her little girl.

Mary's mother was sure of it, and promised to bring one the next day.

That evening when the doctor came to see Janie, he found her very weak, and told her mother that he was afraid she would never run about again; she might live two or three days, or perhaps a week, but each day she was losing strength. The doctor was then told about her great desire to become a Catholic and to see a priest.

"Well, do not thwart her more than you can help," he replied. "Any happiness you can give her will do her good."

When the priest came the next day, Janie's mother saw him first and told him that she was quite willing to do anything that would make her little girl's last days happier.

"She talks of nothing but Mary's church and Mary's priest," said the poor mother, the tears streaming down her face. "'Tis the only religion she knows, so we are quite willing for her to be a Catholic, if it will make her happy."

Then she took him up to Janie's little room, where he sat by the bed and talked to her gently and kindly. He was surprised to find how well the child was instructed, for there was very little Mary had learnt at school, that she had not taught to Janie.

Finding how really anxious she was to be a Catholic so that she might receive Our Dear Lord in Holy Communion, the priest baptised her, heard her simple little confession, and promised to bring her Holy Communion the next morning.

When he was gone, and Janie's father and mother were sitting with her, they could not help noticing the change in Janie's face. It was radiantly happy, and her eyes shone like two big stars.

"Oh, mamma! oh, daddy!" she said, "I am so happy. I do love you for letting me be a Catholic."

That evening Mary's mother came in to show them how to prepare a little altar, and she brought with her a pretty little Rosary that Mary had bought with her own pocket money for Janie; she also brought some roses to put on the altar, promising to come in time for Janie's First Holy Communion the next morning.

About eight o'clock in the morning the priest brought Our Lord to Janie. Mary's mother was there as she had promised, and Janie's father and mother knelt beside the bed. Janie, propped up with pillows, her eyes closed, her hands clasped, looked like a little white lily, as she received her dear Jesus into her heart. For some minutes she prayed fervently, then opening her eyes she smiled sweetly at her father and mother, who were still kneeling near their little daughter, weeping silently.

"Oh, daddy, do not cry," she said, "for I am so happy."

The priest blessed her, promising to come and see her again that day, when he would give her still another Sacrament, called "Extreme Unction."

During the next two days Janie grew weaker and weaker, but she was now perfectly happy; she knew she was dying, but for this was glad, she said, for then she would never stain her soul which Jesus had washed so white in His own Precious Blood.

The second day after her First Holy Communion, the little girl put her arms lovingly round her father and mother when they bent over her.

"Oh, I do love you so," she said, as she kissed them, "but I love Jesus best of all."

That night she fell asleep, and whilst she was sleeping, Jesus came and took her little soul to His beautiful home in heaven.

BOBBIE

Bobbie was just six when he first came to school; the chubbiest and happiest little lad you could wish to see. His father was an actor, and Bobbie had travelled all over the country with him, going to school for a few weeks at a time in the town in which they were staying. But now that he was six, his father thought it best for his little son to remain at one school, where he would be properly taught; so he took some rooms in Liverpool for Bobbie and his mother, and made arrangements for him to enter the convent school.

Bobbie was a friendly little fellow and soon settled down quite happily. Although he was fonder of play than of work, he soon learnt to read and write, and also to say his prayers and Catechism.

Every Monday morning Sister used to ask who had been to Mass the day before, and Bobbie had always to answer "No."

At first, as he was only six, Sister did not worry, but after his seventh birthday she began to get anxious.

"How is it you do not go to Mass?" she inquired. "Does not mother take you with her?"

"Mother doesn't go," he said. "She always has a headache on Sundays. I give her her breakfast in bed, and then I go with Johnny Brown to sail my boat in the park."

"But the church is almost next door to your house. It would be quite easy to hear Mass before you go to play," said Sister.

Bobbie agreed it would, but the following Monday he still had to answer "No" to Sister's usual question.

He was now in the First Confession class, but Sister hesitated about letting him receive this Sacrament, because he still made no attempt to go to Mass on Sundays. Just before the day for the First Confessions, Sister spoke to the priest about him, for you see it was no good Bobbie going to Confession if he was not sorry, and he could not be sorry if he would not try to do his duty. However, the priest asked Sister to send him with the others, and he would have a talk with him.

Bobbie was quite pleased with the idea of going to Confession, and told Sister he'd got plenty of sins ready, and that he expected he would feel quite different when they were all gone.

Sister hoped for the best, and Bobbie thought that once all his sins were gone it would be easier to be good.

So in his turn Bobbie went to Confession, and when he came out his little face looked very serious; he took no notice of the others, but walked quietly up to Our Lady's altar, and kneeling there prayed quietly for some time.

The next Monday when Sister asked who had been to Mass, up went Bobbie's hand.

"Oh, Bobbie, I am pleased," said Sister.

"I am always going now," said Bobbie. "I promised Our Lady that I would never, never miss again."

The promise was kept; for the three years Bobbie remained at that school, he was always present at Holy Mass on Sunday.

Not long after this Bobbie made his First Holy Communion; all the little children's fathers and mothers were there except Bobbie's; his mother had a headache and was in bed, so Bobbie had dressed himself. However, no one was happier than he that day; he entered heart and soul into everything, whether praying in the chapel or playing at the games provided for their amusement. Joy filled his soul and a wonderful love for Our Divine Lord and His Blessed Mother, and Bobbie had great need of all this love, for his mother, finding how faithful Bobbie kept to his duties, how he never neglected his prayers, however late it was or tired he might be, did all she could to prevent him.

On his First Communion Day Bobbie had been given a little Rosary, and each night he said it before getting into bed. Three or four times his mother coming upstairs and finding him kneeling there had pulled him roughly up, and even beaten him, saying she wanted no religion in her house; but the next night would find Bobbie again on his knees, for our Blessed Lord strengthened him in a wonderful way. He had much difficulty, too, in getting to Mass, for once his mother discovered where he went on Sunday mornings, she did her best to prevent it, and though she sometimes prevented his going to Holy Communion, he never once missed Mass; for he had found out a church where he could hear one at twelve o'clock, when his mother thought it too late; and yet this little boy was only eight years old.

In spite of her unkindness to him over his religion, Bobbie loved his mother, and not one word of all she made him suffer was ever told at school, not even to the Sister, who would never have known if the landlady where Bobbie lived had not come up to see if anything could be done to make the little boy's life easier.

Soon after this Bobbie was confirmed, and God the Holy Ghost by His great gift of fortitude helped him to persevere, and so he did until, soon after his tenth birthday, his father coming home and seeing how difficult things were for his little boy, took him away with him.

FRANÇOISE

arie Louise Françoise was born at the castle of Gezaincourt, the home of her grandmother, Madame de Fouquesolles. The following day she was baptised, and given the name of Marie Louise Françoise, as it was the feast day of St Francis. Her grandmother held her at the baptismal font, and soon became so attached to the little one that she begged her mother to allow her to be brought up at the castle. As there were already two other children at home, her mother consented, and the little baby was taken to Gezaincourt, which the grandmother promised should, later on, be given to Françoise for her own.

Madame de Fouquesolles was a very good and fervent Catholic; being so rich, and living in such a beautiful home, she had many servants and tenants who lived on her estate. These she helped in every possible way. They looked up to her as their example, and went to her for advice in all their troubles and difficulties.

Although her grandmother was so devoted to Françoise, she did not spoil her. On the contrary she was very strict, and especially particular about obedience. Françoise had a very strong will of her own, and liked to have her own way, so that at times her grandmother was obliged to punish her.

One morning, when the little grandchild disobeyed her governess, she was told to go as a punishment to the top of the stairs, and remain on the landing till she was sent for. Françoise did not like this penance, so she said to her grandmother:

"If I go there, I shall scream so loud you will tell me to come down again," for she knew her grandmother could not bear much noise.

"You must go all the same," was the reply, "and remain on the landing till you are given permission to come down."

Very unwillingly Françoise began to go up the stairs, saying as she went:

"I will not stop. I shall make too much noise."

At last she arrived at the landing, then opening her mouth she began to scream at the top of her voice, until her grandmother, frightened that she would injure her chest, sent the governess to bring her down.

Françoise was triumphant, and with a smiling face came down the stairs, holding the hand of her governess.

"I told you I should scream," she said, feeling she had conquered.

But her grandmother, calling her to her side, told her of the Little Child Jesus at Nazareth, how happy He made His dear Mother by His obedience and gentleness, but that now He was in heaven, watching the little children whom He loved so dearly. And of how sad it once made Him to see them naughty and disobedient.

The little girl's eyes filled with tears. She had not thought of this; she would not make Him sad again. No, she would go once more to the landing and stay there so quietly that He would be happy again. Then without another word she climbed the stairs a second time and remained for a full half-hour upon the landing, "to make up," as she said afterwards, "for displeasing Little Jesus."

For some time after this Françoise tried to be good, then she forgot all about Little Jesus watching her, and there came another naughty day. There was a certain terrace in the grounds upon which Françoise had been told she must not walk. But just because it was forbidden, Françoise felt a great desire to go there. She went, and was immediately sent for to be punished. The penance over, she went out again, and again returned to the forbidden terrace, saying as she went, "I want to go, so I shall go, just because I want to." Again she was sent for, and the penance repeated, but even this did not stop her. Six times she deliberately returned to the terrace; six times was she brought back to her grandmother to be punished, and only after the last time did the willful child give in.

Françoise very early understood the difference between really willful naughtiness, and what was simply thoughtlessness. One day her grandmother had given her a pair of new shoes ornamented with large rosettes. While she was running near the lake, the rosettes became wet and dirty. Noticing this, her governess began to scold her for spoiling them. But Françoise replied, "Why do you care so much about it? It isn't a sin to dirty rosettes."

Another day while they were out in the garden, Françoise, who was only four years old, was stung by a wasp. She immediately began to scream aloud with the pain. Her governess told her she had much better be quiet and bear the pain for her sins.

"I haven't done any sins yet," the little girl replied, "but I will stop crying for the love of Jesus," and she did.

When Françoise was six years old she was prepared for her first Confession. She told the priest all the sins that she could remember, but to her surprise he only gave her two "Our Fathers" for her penance.

"Fancy," she said to her governess, "only two Our Fathers! Grandmother would have given me a much bigger penance."

But the governess told her that Our Lord had done penance for her when He had shed His Precious Blood during His Bitter Passion, and it was this Precious Blood that cleansed her soul in the Sacrament of Penance.

"Then let me go again," she said. "Only what do people say the second time? Do they offend the Good God again when He has once forgiven them?" And from this time Françoise was never known to be willfully disobedient, though of course she sometimes disobeyed through forgetfulness.

As was said before, her grandmother did not spoil her, but the many visitors who came to stay at this beautiful castle were not so wise. They would tell the little girl how beautiful she

was, praise her for her cleverness, and if her
grandmother had not stopped them would have
ended in making her very vain and proud.

But seeing the danger of leaving Françoise
to their spoiling, she arranged to send her to a
convent school all the summer months. Then,
when winter came and all the visitors had gone,
she would have her home again to live with her.
It was during one of these summer terms at the
convent school that Françoise made her First
Holy Communion. Very carefully did the good
Sisters prepare her for this great Sacrament.
They taught her how to pray well, and how to
fight against her faults, so that every day they
might become fewer. Then for three days before
her First Holy Communion, Françoise went
into retreat; that is, instead of doing lessons
and playing with the other children, she spent
those days in preparing her heart to receive Our
Blessed Lord, listening to the instructions given,
reading the life of Jesus or of His saints, and also
by praying before the Blessed Sacrament in the
convent chapel. She also tried to make her heart
very pure by making a fervent confession, full
of sorrow for the many times she had saddened
Little Jesus by her willfulness and disobedience.

She asked her grandmother and governess also to forgive her for the trouble she had given them.

When the happy day came, with a heart overflowing with joy she offered herself body and soul to Our Blessed Lord. He accepted her offering, and later on, when she was grown up, He asked her to give up all her riches and pleasures, and to come to live with, and work for Him, teaching little children to know and love Him.

Françoise did as He asked. She sold all her great possessions, and with the money helped to build convent schools, where hundreds of children who would otherwise never have known about Almighty God, were taught by her and by others who came to live with her.

A FIRST COMMUNION DAY

It was a week before the First Communion Day when five little children might have been seen seated together engaged in earnest conversation. The eldest, Nita, a dark-haired, dark-eyed girl of eight, was in the middle of the group.

"My heart is full of beautiful flowers for Baby Jesus," she was saying. "But oh! if only I could do some great big thing for Him before next week."

"I should like to do a great big thing too," said a little fair-haired girl of six and a half named Josie. "I did lend my best dollie to Annie yesterday, though I wanted it myself, and I didn't cry when I fell down in the garden and hurt my knee. Those were rather big things."

"Yes, they were all right, but not really big, like the things I mean," answered Nita.

"But Sister said everything we did for Jesus counted," broke in Norah, "and I've done lots and lots of little things to please Him. When Baby

Jesus comes to my heart He will find it full of little daisy flowers."

"I've done things like not talking in class, and trying with my writing," said little Clare. "But I don't always remember, and I haven't done any big ones."

"I wonder if Little Jesus is looking forward to next week. Perhaps He's looking down on us now and seeing which heart He likes best," said Nita. "He always likes to watch us when we are good. Mother says that when we play nicely together, He comes and plays with us, though we can't see Him."

"Does He?" said Josie, much impressed. "Then let's go and play now, and perhaps He will come too."

But at that moment the bell rang, and jumping up, the little group ran to join the others.

A few more days went by. Then came the beautiful Feast of the Annunciation, the 25th March. The Mass was to be at eight o'clock. In good time the chapel was filled to overflowing. In the very front row knelt the little First Communicants in snow-white dresses, wreathes, and veils. Behind them knelt their parents, the rest of the chapel being filled with Sisters and pupils. The altar was beautifully decorated with sweet spring flowers, and during the Mass the organ played, and the pupils sang in honour of the occasion. After the Consecration the little ones said aloud their simple acts before Holy Communion, after which they slowly and reverently approached the altar rails. Returning to their places with their little hands joined and their heads bent low, they knelt so quietly that not one was seen to move.

When Mass was over the priest returned to the sacristy. Still the little ones remained wrapt in prayer. The short acts after Holy Communion were commenced by one of the Sisters. Obediently each little head was raised, and reverently the prayers were repeated, then once more the First Communicants prayed in silence until a signal was given that it was time to leave the chapel.

Down in the big hall the parents were now waiting to see their little ones. At first the children seemed quite shy, but soon they were eagerly showing their First Communion presents— medals, prayer books or Rosaries, with numbers of holy pictures.

Then came breakfast, and during the morning a visit, with the Sister Superior, to each of the

Five little girls eagerly surrounded Sister
anxious to talk over the day's events.

classes of the school. Seeing the happy little faces brought back to the minds of the big girls happy memories of their own First Communion day, now long past. Then there were merry games and happy hours together, with now and again a little visit to chapel, just to thank Our Dear Lord once more for their great privilege and to show Him that He was not forgotten.

The day ended with Benediction, during which the little ones read aloud an Act of Consecration to Our Lady, asking her to help them always to keep their hearts pure and white for Little Jesus.

Soon after this the children's parents had to return home. When the last good-byes had been said, the five little girls eagerly gathered round Sister, anxious once more for her to admire their presents, and to talk over events of the day.

"Sister," said Nita, "Josie told us she couldn't think of anything to say when she came back from the altar this morning."

Little Josie's face flushed with shame, but looking up shyly at Sister she said, "I did talk to Jesus after the prayers, but at first I could only keep hugging Him tight, and saying, 'Dear Little Jesus, I do love You' over and over again, but after the prayers I said 'Hail Maries' for everybody."

"That was a beautiful thanksgiving, Josie," said Sister. "Little Jesus likes so much to hear you tell Him that you love Him."

"I told Him I loved Him, Sister," said Norah, "and I told Him the story of St. Gerard, and said I would come and talk to Him when He was lonely too, like St. Gerard did."

"I told Jesus about Blessed Julie, and I told Him my brother teased me, and I told Him all about the flowers I had put in my heart for Him," said Nita.

"Oh! I forgot all about the flowers," broke in Clare, "but He would have seen them, wouldn't He, Sister? "

"I told Jesus about mother being ill, and asked Him to make her better," said Agnes, who had been very disappointed that her parents had been unable to be present that day. "And I asked Him to help me with my reading and sums."

"Little Jesus has answered part of your prayer already," said Sister, "for a letter came this evening to say that mother was better and that daddy hoped she would soon be quite well again, and able to come and see her little girl."

"Oh, Sister! isn't He good?" replied Agnes. "May we go to Holy Communion again to-morrow, so that I may thank Him?"

"Now that you have made your First Holy Communion, you may all go every day just like the other girls, only you will talk to Him and not leave Him alone when He comes, won't you?" answered Sister.

"Oh, yes! indeed we will," they all exclaimed.

"Every night when I go to bed I shall try to think of something nice to tell Little Jesus," said Josie. "I want Him to like coming into my heart best of all."

"So shall I," chimed in each of the others.

Just then the bell rang for supper, after which five tired, but very happy, little children were soon fast asleep in bed.